Cultivate Millionaires

MOM, I WILL BE RICH!

 Instill Habits Early
Achieve Financial Freedom Young

S U M M E R   P H A M

Cover design and typesetting by Studio Heta

First Edition

ISBN: 979-8-9935227-1-5

Table of Contents

Introduction 1

PART 1: Foundation to Cultivate the Seed

1. **The First Step to Having Anything** | *The Power of Wealth Conditioning* 9
2. **Lobsters From Maine** | *The High Standards Advantage* 19
3. **Good Things Come to Those Who Appreciate** | *The Appreciation Advantage* 27
4. **Build Discipline and Slap Your Lower Self** | *The Discipline Advantage* 35
5. **Be Batman** | *Strategic Dream Cultivation* 43
6. **High Price Tag** | *The Self-Worth Principle* 51
7. **Be Delusionally Confident** | *The Confidence Formula* 59

PART 2: Fundamental Habits

8. **Good Habits Pay Off** | *The Habit Installation Framework* 71
9. **Collect Rocks** | *The Acquisition Mindset* 85
10. **Build a Tent** | *The Resourcefulness Mindset* 93
11. **Don't Wait for the Eggs to Boil** | *The Optimization Practice* 99
12. **Have Good Taste** | *The Quality Recognition System* 105
13. **What's Good for You IS Good** | *The Beneficial Preference Shift* 113
14. **Be Picky with People Like You're Picky with Food** | *The Strategic Association Principle* 119
15. **Don't Be Nice** | *The Good Over Nice Approach* 131
16. **Get What You Want** | *The Diplomatic Influence Principle* 139
17. **Count 1, 2, 3** | *The Emotional Sovereignty Principle* 147
18. **You'll Lose If You Let Your Emotion Win** | *The Emotional Control Framework* 155
19. **Cheapest Lessons** | *The Vicarious Learning Advantage* 163
20. **Celebration Penalty** | *The Celebration Equilibrium* 171
21. **Showing Off Is for Losers** | *The Authentic Validation Principle* 179
22. **Treat Your Body Like a Temple** | *The Ultimate Priority Principle* 187

PART 3: Formula for Success & Freedom

23. **You Need to Be an Expert** | *The Informed Client Advantage* 199
24. **Dominate** | *The Identity Specialization Strategy* 209
25. **A Left-Hand Job** | *The Strategic Security System* 215
26. **Think Long Enough and You Shall Receive** | *The Intentional Attraction System* 223
27. **Formula for Success** | *The Universal Achievement Formula* 231
28. **Take the Bullet Train** | *The Mentor Acceleration System* 239
29. **If You Don't Have This, You Won't Get It** | *The Motivational Clarity Principle* 247
30. **Roadmap to Getting RICH** | *The Wealth Construction Blueprint* 255
31. **Front-Load** | *The Front-Loading Advantage* 265
32. **Create Your Own Club** | *The Self-Creation Principle* 275

PART 4: Be Better and Achieving Excellence

33. **Rewire** | *The Wisdom Discernment System* 287
34. **Not Everything Applies 100%** | *The Application Intelligence Principle* ... 295
35. **Be Attractive. Don't Be Unattractive** | *The Value Surplus Principle* ... 303
36. **Kaizen!** | *The Incremental Excellence System* 309
37. **Be Better Than the Previous Generation** | *The Generational Advancement Principle* 317
38. **Pass It Forward** | *The Contribution Culmination* 325

What's Next? 337
Acknowledgements 339
Index 341
About the Author 343

Introduction

Choosing between the $2.99 and $2.49 lettuce. Settling for budget hotels instead of staying where you really want. Living paycheck to paycheck and making financial compromises every single day.

This is no way to live.

Money isn't about counting dollars—it's about freedom. Financial freedom gives you control over your time, choices, and life. It allows you to walk away from situations that don't serve you and access experiences that genuinely matter.

Imagine a life where abundance isn't aspirational—it's your reality.

The question isn't whether to achieve financial freedom. It's WHEN. And the answer should be: as early as possible.

Dan Lok asks it bluntly: "Why the F would you want to get rich slow?"

Why wait until seventy to retire when your body can't fully enjoy it? Your thirties and forties—when you have energy, health, and decades ahead— these are your prime years when freedom matters most.

Building a strong financial foundation early—in your twenties and thirties—compounds into exponential advantages later. It's absolutely okay to want a good life for yourself and for your children.

Why I Wrote This Book

"Mom, I'm rich!" Max exclaimed, counting his New Year's money with excitement. "I'm a billionaire!"

"Do you have a billion dollars?" I asked, amused.

"Not yet," he replied confidently. "But I'm going to be rich when I grow up, so I can buy lots of toys and chocolate. I'm going to be a billionaire."

Like most children, mine want everything they encounter. The inevitable negotiations at checkout—"You can only pick one"—always follow. My husband would often explain the fundamental truth: "You need money to buy the things you want. You have to work hard and earn enough so you can."

At age six and (barely) three, they're already dreamers. They start connecting ideas quickly.

They study my travel photography with longing. "I want to go here," they say, pointing. "Mama, take me to Paris," Max insists, captivated by my Eiffel Tower photograph.

"I want to travel everywhere in the world. I'll take you when I grow up," he promises with remarkable certainty.

"Can we go to Croatia again? Can we go to Gotham City?" Someone is a Batman fan.

Watching them dream sparked something in me.

I want to give my children a genuine head start—a life defined by abundance rather than constraints. I want to give my children music lessons, taekwondo training, dance classes—every enriching opportunity. I want to travel with them, live in excellent school districts, and provide the finest education available.

Don't you want the same for yours?

I wrote this book because of my children—and for parents who want their children to achieve financial freedom early.

If you're in your fifties, let's be honest—the boat for getting rich young has sailed. But plenty of people built wealth later in life—Colonel Sanders launched his empire in his sixties.

Even if you feel you've missed the window personally, you can still change the trajectory for your children and future generations.

As Proverbs 13:22 states, "A good man leaves an inheritance to his children's children."

You're reading this book because I believe you want to give your children a better life than you had—financially, mentally, and emotionally. You want them to have options, freedom, and opportunity early in life, equipping them with the tools to live full, happy lives.

I've built my own freedom—not at the pinnacle of wealth, but enough to understand its accessibility, especially when you start early. I refuse to let my children miss this opportunity, and I want the same for your family.

My success isn't of a magnitude that has made me a prominent figure. I'm just a regular person; I wasn't born into wealth, but I was fortunate enough to discover certain principles early on. I consider myself remarkably lucky to have encountered these fundamentals and achieved my success. Had I possessed this clarity even earlier, I would have pursued it with ten times the intensity. That's precisely why I'm determined to instill these wealth-building habits in my children from the start.

This book is my public commitment—a promise that real freedom doesn't have to be postponed for another generation.

Who This Book Is For

This book is for those who understand that achieving financial freedom isn't hoped for—it's built.

It's for parents who want their children to grow up financially free.

It's for those who care less about managing behavior in the moment and more about shaping discipline, confidence, character, and financial independence over time.

For parents who believe:

- You are the first environment your children grow up in
- Environment matters more than instructions
- Standards matter more than motivation
- What is normalized at home quietly becomes a child's baseline

You want your children to grow up:

- Expecting financial freedom as a baseline, not an aspiration
- Comfortable around money, opportunity, and success
- Disciplined enough to delay gratification and compound effort
- Capable of building real wealth, not just earning income
- Grounded in character, responsibility, and self-respect
- Held to standards that protect, multiply, and preserve their success

It's not for those who believe money doesn't matter, or that wealth should be postponed until "later in life."

It's not for those looking for shortcuts, gimmicks, or one-off tactics.

This book is for those who are intentional about transformation and the legacy they create.

Let's Clarify a Few Things:

- Money solves way more problems than poverty does. While money can't guarantee happiness, neither does poverty. It's perfectly okay to want a higher quality of life. Exceptional experiences come more easily with money, and generosity flows more naturally when you have extra.

- I don't claim to have invented these principles. They're proven—I've simply made them accessible and translated them into plain English and practical application—the same principles I'm teaching my children and sharing with families seeking abundance.

- This book is not an investment manual; there are many books like that. No strategy works without the right foundation. Think of this book as financial nutrition, not a single recipe. These principles can be applied to any wealth-building method you choose.

- The goal and key distinction here is not just achieving financial freedom, but achieving it early, and enjoying a higher quality of life sooner.

- If any financially independent individual tells you these fundamentals are steering you wrong, ask them to contact me, and I'll refund you.

- The Teach & Thrive section at the end of each chapter provides practical ways to apply these principles to parenting. If you develop your own methods, please share them with our community. We're all here to prepare our children for a brighter, more abundant future.

- I recommend reading this book in order. Don't jump around—each principle builds upon the previous one. This isn't a one-time read—it's a lifestyle guide for a lifetime journey.

Before You Read Further

This book is written primarily for parents—yet its principles serve anyone committed to raising financially free children or becoming financially free themselves.

Children are not shaped by instructions. They are shaped by conditioning and what is normalized around them.

The standards you live by.
The expectations you set.
The environment you create.

That is how discipline, confidence, character, and financial freedom are formed.

Read what follows with that lens.

This is not about managing moments.
It is about shaping conditions over time.

PART 1

Foundation to Cultivate the Seed

The First Step to Having Anything

*"You can't hit a target
you cannot see,
and you cannot see a target
you do not have."*

– Zig Ziglar

The first step in attaining anything is knowing it exists and wanting it. To obtain anything, you must first be aware of what's possible.

Being immersed in environments of abundance provides glimpses of what a genuinely fulfilling life looks like. This sparks dreams and goals, leading to ways to achieve them.

Picture this: You're ten years old, somehow crammed into the back seat of a five-seater Mercedes with your family of five, plus the driver and his wife. (Physics clearly worked differently in the 90s)

The Vins are our family chauffeurs to what can only be described as "Lifestyles of the Rich and Famous: Kid Edition." We're climbing these pristine, tree-lined roads in San Diego where even the air smells EXPENSIVE. You know that smell—like success mixed with patchouli, bergamot, and the faint scent of "we-don't-shop-at-dollar-stores."

Mrs. Vin emerges from their Mercedes like she's stepping off a movie set, in her wrinkle-free, structured dress and dripping in diamonds. Mr. Vin performs a ritual where he carefully unscrews the iconic hood ornament before going in. (Yes, I just dated myself—back when Mercedes had detachable hood ornaments because apparently car theft was classier in the 90s.)

The Accidental Millionaire Mindset

Let me start with the obligatory humble beginnings story, but I'll keep it short because, honestly, you've heard this before: Girl born poor, parents worked for below minimum wage—standard poor story stuff.

But here's where my story gets interesting, and here's where LUCK played its first hand: Even though my parents were poor, they had rich friends. And those wealthy friends had networks of other wealthy friends.

Mr. and Mrs. Vin lived in what my child-mind considered pure luxury—a house perched on the San Diego hills. Inside their home, I was mesmerized by things I'd never seen: elegant curtains that probably cost more than our annual income, and a massive 50-inch television that dominated their living room, along with other systems, like entertainment venues. This was the early '90s, people. Fifty inches might as well have been a movie theater.

But the real show-stopper? Hearing Mr. Vin casually mention to my parents that they made $100,000.

I still remember the moment. My parents were sitting at their kitchen table, and Mrs. Vin was pouring tea while Mr. Vin said, almost offhandedly, "Business is good this year—our stores' revenue has increased." I specifically heard ONE HUNDRED THOUSAND dollars. I was too young to know if that was in a day, a month, or a year. That number—$100,000—became my first financial goal. Not because it was smart or strategic, but because it was the only number I'd ever heard that sounded like BIG and real money. That was an enormous amount to me at the time. (Spoiler alert: I should have aimed WAY higher, but we'll talk about that in Principle 5.)

The Vietnamese Parent Olympics

The Vins owned several 7-Eleven stores and gas stations near the beach. More importantly, their children were headed to medical residency, just like every other kid in their social circle.

Let me paint you a picture of a typical Vietnamese gathering of friends and family: Imagine a room full of parents where every conversation is basically a competitive sport called "My Kid Is Going to Be More Successful Than Your Kid." The gold medal winner? Anyone whose child is pursuing a career as a medical doctor.

"Mrs. Nguyen's son just got into UCSD medical school."

"Oh, really? Well, Mrs. Tran's daughter is doing her residency at UCLA."

"That's nice, but did you hear about Mrs. Le's boy? He's specializing in neurosurgery."

Every single parent gathering turned into "Dr. So-and-So's Son/Daughter Achievement Hour." You'd get sick of hearing that word. Doctor. Doctor. Doctor.

If you're Vietnamese and you're not becoming a doctor, you're basically the family's black sheep. Fine, maybe not the black sheep, but your parents definitely won't have bragging rights at the next gathering. One of my parents' friends has five children, all of whom are doctors. All five children! And those children married doctors, too. That's just ridiculous! That mom really deserves a lot of bragging trophies.

The Vins' kids? Getting ready for medical residency. Their friends? Doctors and lawyers. Every conversation somehow circled back to someone's child in the medical field. By the time you're twelve, you either commit to medical school or accept your fate as the family disappointment who chose... gasp... BUSINESS.

This environment didn't just influence me—it shaped my brother's entire life trajectory. He absorbed the doctor discussions and decided in middle school that he was going to be a physician. Every class he took, every extracurricular activity, every academic choice became a calculated stepping stone toward medical school. Apparently, some people actually have their career figured out at age twelve.

But here's where my child-mind brain got permanently rewired...

The Beach Event That Changed Everything

The Vins took us to this company event that looked like someone took Pinterest, gave it an unlimited budget, and said, "Make it happen." We're talking about white tablecloth setups that stretch for what seemed like a mile. Ice sculptures that probably cost more than our monthly rent. A charcuterie station that could feed a small country.

And the fruit display seemed like a mountain of fruit varieties that would put Whole Foods to shame. Well-dressed people walking around like this level of abundance was just... Tuesday.

There I am, standing there thinking, "HOW did these people make it here? What do they do?" I remember thinking, "I want to live in *this* world."

> **Plot twist: That moment of childhood awe became my financial GPS for life.**

The Accidental Genius of Wealth Conditioning

Here's what most parents don't realize: You cannot pursue what you don't know exists.

It's like trying to find Waldo when you don't know what Waldo looks like.

That childhood exposure to the Vins' world—their casual business-success talk, their Mercedes lifestyle, their "doctor children" achievements— planted seeds in my child mind that grew into my own financial success story.

> But here's the kicker: This happens whether
> you're intentional about it or not.

Your children are absorbing wealth conditioning RIGHT NOW. The question is: What kind of conditioning are they getting?

If they're hearing "we can't afford that" and "money doesn't grow on trees," guess what their financial thermostat is being set to? If they're seeing you stress over every purchase decision, what kind of money relationship are they learning?

The Wealth Conditioning Reality Check

Being around the Vins wasn't just about seeing nice things—it was about normalizing a different level of thinking. When everyone in their circle discussed investments, business decisions, and achievement goals, that became my norm too.

This isn't about showing your kids expensive cars so they'll want expensive cars. It's about showing them that OPTIONS exist. It's about exposing them to environments where people have CHOICES—about where to live, where to travel, how to spend their time, and how to solve problems. When you see someone effortlessly pick up a dinner check for eight people, you don't just notice the money. You notice the ease. The lack of stress. The *ability* to be generous without calculation.

It's the difference between raising kids who think "we can't afford that" versus kids who automatically ask, "HOW can we afford that?"

Most people spend their entire lives trapped by the limitations programmed into their minds when they were young. But what if we could be *more* intentional about that programming?

Your Strategic Exposure Assignment

Start exposing yourself and your children to environments where financial success is the norm, not the exception. I'm not talking about putting on airs or pretending to be something you're not. I'm talking about strategic conditioning.

Visit upscale neighborhoods. Eat occasionally at restaurants where successful people gather (even if it's just appetizers—your wallet will thank you). Browse fancy supercar showrooms. If that feels intimidating, start with Tesla showrooms—they're designed for browsing. Attend free entrepreneurship lectures.

The goal isn't materialism or keeping up with the Joneses. It's expanding your children's concept of what's POSSIBLE and planting seeds of ambition that will drive their future choices.

Because here's the truth: When you see nice cars and beautiful environments, your children naturally wonder, "What do these people do? How did they achieve this?" It's not about the THINGS themselves—it's about the OPTIONS successful people have and HOW they created those options.

The Bottom Line

The first step in attaining anything is knowing it exists and wanting it. To have good things, you must first be aware of what's possible.

You can't reach a destination you don't know exists. You can't search for something if you don't know what it looks like.

Begin by exposing yourself and your children to high-quality environments, enriching experiences, successful individuals, and ambitious goals. Dreams lead to goals, goals lead to action, and action makes dreams a reality.

Exposure beats explanation every single time. You can lecture your kids about financial success until you're blue in the face, but thirty minutes in the right environment will do more for their wealth conditioning than thirty hours of "money talk."

Curious if I eventually hit that $100,000 goal? Or if my brother actually became a doctor? Keep reading. But the key point is this: my parents didn't deliberately expose us to this "wealth conditioning," but it happened anyway and profoundly shaped our aspirations.

So thank you, Mr. and Mrs. Vin, for accidentally giving me a masterclass in wealth conditioning. (And yes, I still wonder how seven people fit in that Mercedes.)

"Desire is the starting point of all achievement."

—*Napoleon Hill*

Principle 1: **The Power of Wealth Conditioning**

Deliberately expose yourself and your children to environments of abundance. If you don't know something exists, you won't even know you desire it, let alone pursue it. Early conditioning toward wealth and opportunity plants powerful seeds of ambition and direction that last a lifetime.

◉ Teach & Thrive

Here are five strategic ways to condition your children for wealth (no Mercedes required):

1. **Possibility Tours:** Take monthly "exploration trips" to upscale neighborhoods, luxury hotels, or innovation centers. Frame it as "seeing how different people live." Grab tea at the Ritz lobby, walk through a Tesla showroom, and visit model homes in premium communities. The goal? Making excellence feel normal, not mystical.

2. **Success Story Immersion:** Introduce your children to accomplished people through free university lectures, community business events, or author book signings. Prepare questions beforehand so your child can engage meaningfully. When success has a face and a story, it becomes achievable rather than abstract.

3. **Language Conditioning:** Replace "we can't afford it" with "that's not our priority right now" or "how could we create money for this?" When children hear abundance-focused language consistently, they develop abundance-focused thinking automatically. This subtle shift teaches that money is about choices and priorities, not limitations.

4. **Possible Boards:** Create a family "possible board" featuring extraordinary achievements, inspiring innovations, and beautiful destinations. Include a dedicated space for each child's specific dreams. This environmental cue reinforces expansive thinking during their most impressionable years.

5. **Success Story Sharing:** Share stories of people who built wealth through various paths—entrepreneurs, investors, professionals. Watch age-appropriate documentaries (or read biographies) about innovators, entrepreneurs, and visionaries. Follow with family discussions about what impressed them and what they might do similarly. This builds entrepreneurial thinking patterns naturally.

Remember: You're not trying to spoil your children or create materialistic monsters. You're expanding their mental model of what's possible so they can dream bigger, plan better, and achieve more than you ever imagined.

PRINCIPLE 2

Lobsters From Maine

"I like to eat lobster directly from Maine,
and I like to see bullfights in sunny old Spain."

—Frank Sinatra, *"Nothing But the Best"*

Frank Sinatra knew something most people miss: **You get what you settle for.**

Setting high standards is like putting yourself on the exclusive guest list. No bad vibes, uninspiring friends, or cold French fries allowed! With high standards, you get an automatic shield against nonsense—and a rocket strapped to your back, launching you toward the good stuff.

It's perfectly okay to be that person with standards so high that even your coffee needs a background check.

The Great Standards Reality Check

The standards you set for yourself become the baseline you accept. Your standards determine the quality of your life—every area of it. The environment you choose, the treatment you accept from others, the way you present yourself to the world. For example, if you let "being a mom" become your excuse to wear stained sweats and skip the mirror, you'll start showing up everywhere looking like a broken-down bus instead of a Ferrari—and thinking that's just normal.

Here's the thing about standards—they're like a personal filter system. Whatever quality you set as your baseline becomes your magnetic attraction point. **You *see* what you look for. You *get* what you settle for.**

What are the consequences of having low standards? It's like starting out wanting the handsome, rich guy, but somewhere along the line you settle—and now you're splitting the bill and calling it independence.

Think I'm being dramatic? Let me paint you a picture.

The Standards Domino Effect

Ever wonder why vanilla ice cream—*vanilla*, the most basic flavor known to humanity—has more ingredients than a chemistry experiment? It should take exactly five things: milk, sugar, vanilla, cream, and maybe eggs.

That's what happens when we collectively accept LOW STANDARDS.

Same with French fries. Potatoes + real fat (tallow) + salt = perfection. However, fast food fries contain ingredients I can't even pronounce (maybe some of them glow in the dark.)

Here's the plot twist: This isn't just about food.

When everyone accepts mediocrity, mediocrity becomes the norm. When businesses can get away with cheap substitutes and chemical shortcuts, they will. When people don't demand better, better disappears from the menu entirely.

But imagine if *everyone* had high standards. If every consumer said, "Nah, I'll pass on the frozen chemical masquerading as ice cream." If every business actually took pride in its products instead of just its profit margins.

This principle extends beyond food. Imagine if every business operated with uncompromising standards—products and services would improve dramatically. When you hold yourself to a higher code, certain behaviors become simply *beneath you*. Actions that compromise your integrity—you simply won't let them stain your character. It's not that you *can't* be late— it's that punctual people don't do that. It's not that you *can't* leave dirty dishes in the sink for days—it's that organized people have systems.

If every individual upheld high personal standards, societal problems would naturally diminish. The world would transform.

So YES. If *everyone* had high standards, the world would be a better place.

And that transformation starts with you setting higher standards in the six areas that **E.N.R.I.C.H.** your life:

- **Experiences**—the quality of what you allow into your life, including the expectation you set for how you want to be treated and the environments you choose to be in.
- **Network**—the people you surround yourself with.
- **Representation**—how you carry yourself and how you dress (this isn't vanity—it's self-respect). The world treats you the way you present yourself.
- **Identity**—how you identify yourself. You become what you believe.
- **Consumption**—the quality of food you put in your body and what you feed your brain.
- **Habits**—the standards and habits you hold yourself to (because "I'm just not a morning person" isn't a personality trait).

My Standards Boot Camp

Working at IBM elevated my standards to a whole new level—surrounded by people who wouldn't accept anything less than excellence.

During a project for Time Inc. in New York, our IBM Partner took the team to a high-end steakhouse in Manhattan. One of the executives casually mentioned, "Franz has impeccable taste, so if you're picking a restaurant for a team dinner with him, make sure it's the best."

That stuck with me. Then one day, I watched one of the guys change from tennis shoes to dress shoes at his desk. A manager commented, "Franz expects everyone to present their best—you can wear your tennis shoes to get here, but change to your nice pair when you're in the office." "Always dress a little better than the clients."

What further upgraded my standards was reading IBM's core values—*dedication to every client's success, innovation that matters for our company and for the world, and trust and personal responsibility in all relationships*—these weren't just words on a poster. They were lived daily. This didn't just raise my professional standards; it raised my standards for EVERYTHING.

That's when I realized: **high standards aren't restrictive—they're liberating.** They tell you exactly what you're worth and what you should accept. Nothing less.

One of the former IBMers told me with a grin, "It's better to be at IBM than at Microsoft. You know what IBM stands for? It Beats Microsoft." That pretty much summed up the culture—confident, competitive, and unapologetically committed to excellence.

The Self-Standards Revolution

You start identifying as someone who values quality, and suddenly, quality becomes your default setting.

When you set high standards for yourself, you'll set them for the people in your life, too—so you're less likely to be mistreated, because you won't allow it. In fact, never let anyone mistreat you in any way.

The power lies not only in setting high standards for external things, but also in setting high standards for yourself. People with high self-standards continuously strive for improvement and tend to achieve more naturally. This builds genuine self-confidence, which we'll explore further in later chapters.

High Standards = Negative-Experience Proof Armor

Think of high standards as your personal bouncer. They don't let the riffraff into the VIP section of your life. Bad experiences? "Sorry, not on the list." Toxic people? "Nope, dress code violation." Mediocre opportunities? "We're at capacity."

High standards don't just improve your life—they protect it from everything that would drag it down.

The Standards Challenge

Here's your assignment: For the next week, raise your standards in ONE area by just 10%. Maybe it's the quality of food you buy. Perhaps it's how you present yourself when you leave the house. Maybe it's refusing to accept "close enough" in your work.

Watch what happens. Because when you upgrade your standards, everything else in your life mysteriously starts upgrading too.

High Standards = High Quality Life (It's really that simple.)

Principle 2: **The High Standards Advantage**

Set and maintain elevated standards in everything you do. Maintaining high standards for your surroundings, relationships, and personal conduct fosters both protection and prosperity.

◉ Teach & Thrive

Here are five powerful ways to help your children develop high standards:

1. **The Quality Detective Game:** Transform grocery shopping into a learning adventure. Compare ingredients between premium and standard products—show them why some yogurt has five ingredients while others have 25. Let them taste the difference between fresh bread and processed alternatives. Make it fun: "Can you guess which one will make your body stronger?"

2. **Friend Quality Assessment:** Create a family "friendship values" chart listing qualities that matter: honesty, kindness, reliability, and encouragement. When your child faces friendship challenges, reference this chart: "Does this person show the qualities we value?" This builds relationship discernment without judgment.

3. **Excellence Training:** Establish the family practice of "doing it once, doing it right." Whether setting the table or completing homework, encourage thoroughness over shortcuts. Say: "If we need to redo it, we've wasted time. Let's meet our standards the first time." This builds pride in quality work.

4. **Presentation Practice:** Create age-appropriate self-care routines that emphasize self-respect over vanity. For younger children: proper

grooming and clean, appropriate clothing. For older children, discuss how presentation affects confidence and how different situations require varying standards of performance. This builds internal value recognition.

5. **Standards Vocabulary:** Develop family language around standards. Ask: "Is this up to our family standards?" or "What standard would you give this from 1-10?" This creates automatic evaluation frameworks that become lifelong decision-making tools.

Remember: You're not creating perfectionists—you're creating people who know they deserve better and aren't afraid to expect it.

PRINCIPLE 3

Good Things Come to Those Who Appreciate

"Gratitude is the healthiest of all human emotions. The more you express gratitude for what you have, the more likely you will have even more to express gratitude for."

—Zig Ziglar

The more you genuinely appreciate, the more you receive. This isn't some woo-woo manifestation magic—it's basic human psychology with a side of universal justice. Practice gratitude daily and watch your life transform.

But here's what most people get wrong about gratitude...

They think it's about sitting in a lotus position, humming "Kumbaya," and listing three things they're thankful for while their life falls apart around them. That's gratitude lite—the decaf version.

Real appreciation is a full-contact sport.

The Appreciation Advantage

When you truly appreciate something, you naturally take better care of it. You pay attention to it. You invest in it. You make it last. And funny thing—the universe notices people who appreciate what they have and tends to send them more.

It's like being a good friend. When someone genuinely appreciates your friendship, values your time, and shows gratitude for your efforts, don't you want to do *more* for them? The universe operates on the same principle.

But people who don't appreciate? They're energy vampires. They take and take and wonder why good things stop flowing their way.

This principle seems simple, but its depth is often overlooked. Appreciation isn't just about verbally acknowledging good things—it's a complete orientation toward life that fundamentally changes how you experience and receive.

Feeling blessed and fortunate creates positive energy. When you genuinely appreciate, your entire attitude improves, and you become naturally happier. Happy, appreciative people are magnetic; they attract more opportunities, connections, and abundance. Daily gratitude practice fosters resilience, enabling you to navigate challenges with greater perspective and strength.

There are countless small joys and conveniences we take for granted. The concept of appreciation is intuitive, yet many people never master the art of feeling genuinely grateful for their countless blessings.

Some dismiss appreciation practices as ineffective, asking: "How does being thankful change my ACTUAL problems?" But it does—profoundly. The transformation isn't just from the act of listing things you're grateful for, though that's valuable. The real power comes when appreciation becomes an integral part of your character, as natural as breathing.

Genuine appreciation extends beyond gratitude for positive events. It encompasses appreciating all dimensions of life—resources, people, possessions, experiences, and time itself. When you genuinely appreciate, you perceive everything differently and value what you have and who's in your life.

Appreciation Levels: From Amateur to Expert

Level 1: Resource Appreciation

This is kindergarten-level gratitude. Don't pull half a roll of paper towels to wipe your slightly damp hands. Turn off the water while brushing your teeth. (Yes, I'm looking at you, the person who lets the faucet run like Niagara Falls while brushing.)

It's not about being cheap—it's about recognizing that waste is disrespectful. When you waste resources, you're basically telling the universe, "I don't need to value it." What message does that send about your worthiness to receive more? Think of it this way…would you feed someone caviar and wagyu if they only appreciate precooked frozen shrimp and processed patties?

Level 2: Tangible Thing Appreciation

Wasteful people appreciate less; frugal people generally appreciate more. When you purchase items you genuinely value, you naturally appreciate and take better care of them. Impulsive, unconsidered buying typically results in less appreciation and quicker disposal.

When you genuinely appreciate your possessions, you learn to maintain them properly, which significantly extends their lifespan. Identical items might last decades in one household but barely survive a year in another. The difference isn't in the items—it's in the appreciation of their owners.

Level 3: People Appreciation

Consider my situation with my parents babysitting my children. Understanding their role clearly—ensuring safety, providing meals, and basic care—allows me to appreciate everything beyond that as a bonus. They're not responsible for discipline or educational development—that's my job as a parent.

With this clarity, I'm genuinely grateful for their help rather than disappointed when they don't parent exactly as I would. This perspective generates appreciation instead of frustration.

When you're aware of what others contribute and maintain realistic expectations, you feel blessed and fortunate. This naturally expresses itself in how you interact with them. Without clear expectations, disappointment creeps in, leading to adverse reactions that damage relationships.

People who don't appreciate tend to be unhappy, see the world through a negative lens, and experience more unfavorable outcomes as a result. Their lack of appreciation creates a self-reinforcing cycle—negative perception leads to negative behavior, which triggers negative treatment from others, further confirming their pessimistic worldview.

Level 4: Experience Appreciation

Recognize your good fortune when you get to travel. Be grateful when someone introduces you to an opportunity, or when circumstances align in your favor. People who approach life with appreciation naturally share their "lucky" stories, which attract more favorable circumstances. Others become eager to create more positive experiences for appreciative people. After all, who doesn't enjoy making a genuine difference in someone's life?

Valuing possessions fosters frugality and resource mindfulness. Valuing effort and people develops the ability to recognize service and kindness.

When you appreciate someone's hospitality or generosity, you're likely to be welcomed back repeatedly.

Level 5: Time Appreciation

Time is your most non-renewable resource. You can make more money, buy new things, meet new people—but you can't manufacture more time. The entire purpose of this book is to develop wealth habits that enable you to achieve financial freedom *early*, allowing you to spend more time doing the things you love.

When you truly appreciate time, you stop wasting it on things that don't matter. You become intentional. You invest it wisely. And somehow, you end up with MORE of it because you're not throwing it away on nonsense.

The Appreciation Multiplication Effect

Here's the remarkable part: the *more* you appreciate, the more you *have* to appreciate. It's like compound interest for happiness.

Appreciate others' home-cooked meals, and suddenly you're the person people want to cook for. Appreciate your friend's favor, and they will think of you when good opportunities arise. Appreciate your current job, and better positions mysteriously appear.

My Kids' Appreciation Training

I teach my children to say "Thank you, Mom, for cooking" even if they don't love the specific dish. They can say, "Thank you for cooking. I don't love this particular egg—may I have pancakes instead?" When something good happens in our favor, say, "I'm so lucky that..."

It's not about fake enthusiasm. It's about recognizing effort and intention, separate from personal preference.

We practice: "Only take what you'll eat, and eat what you take." Not because we can't afford more food, but because waste is disrespect for the resource, the effort, and the people who don't have enough.

Your Appreciation Upgrade Challenge

For one week, become a gratitude detective. Find something to genuinely appreciate in every situation—yes, even the annoying ones. The slow cashier who's probably dealing with demanding customers all day. That traffic jam is giving you extra time to think. The difficult person who's teaching you patience.

Watch how this simple shift changes not just your mood, but your actual experiences.

Because here's the secret: **The universe is in favor of those who appreciate it.**

Principle 3: **The Appreciation Advantage**

Genuine appreciation creates a virtuous cycle of abundance. When you deeply value what you have—resources, relationships, possessions, experiences, and time—you naturally attract more to appreciate. The more you appreciate, the more you HAVE to appreciate.

◉ Teach & Thrive

Here are five ways to cultivate genuine appreciation in your children:

1. **Resource Awareness Challenge:** Create fun conservation games—who can brush teeth using the least water? Who can create something useful from recycling materials? When resources are temporarily unavailable (due to power outages, etc.), highlight their value when they are available.

2. **Effort Recognition Rituals:** Before meals, take turns sharing one thing you appreciate about the food—the person who prepared it, the farmers who grew it, or specific flavors you enjoy. This creates mindfulness around consumption without feeling forced. Make it genuine, not performative.

3. **Time Value Training:** Use "time jars" with 24 marbles representing daily hours. Remove marbles for sleeping, school, and essentials, then discuss how to invest the remaining "time marbles" wisely. This makes abstract time concepts tangible for children.

4. **Gratitude Currency System:** Create a reward system where children earn "appreciation coins" for genuine expressions of gratitude—not just saying thanks, but also showing care for possessions, helping

others, or recognizing efforts. These coins can be exchanged for special privileges or activities.

5. **Daily Appreciation Practice:** Each morning, family members share this simple statement: "I'm grateful to be alive, safe, and healthy. Today will be a good day." This simple ritual wires gratitude into their identity rather than making it an occasional activity. Consistency creates character.

Goal: Raise children who appreciate abundance when they have it and create more through their grateful attitude.

PRINCIPLE 4

Build Discipline and Slap Your Lower Self

"Through discipline comes freedom."

—*Aristotle*

Self-discipline is the key difference between people who achieve their dreams and those who merely dream. It's the ability to do what needs to be done, when it needs to be done, whether you feel like it or not.

And let's be honest: most of the time, you won't feel like it. But all success is the result of being disciplined enough to do what needs to be done—even when you don't want to.

Discipline isn't punishment—it's freedom training.

This principle reveals why seemingly unrelated habits predict success. The person who makes their bed each morning, organizes their workspace, and fulfills small commitments is developing the fundamental muscle that enables major achievements.

"How you do one thing is how you do everything." The person who's always "running thirty minutes late" is probably cutting corners in other areas of life. Individuals who frequently make late credit card payments are also likely to experience late rent payments.

Areas of Discipline to Master:

Discipline Area #1: Master Prioritization Discipline (Do Hard Things First)

Always tackle the most critical, difficult tasks first. When you front-load the challenging tasks, you accomplish them while your energy and focus are at their strongest. Plus, everything else feels easy by comparison. It's like eating vegetables before dessert—except the vegetables are "call that difficult client" and dessert is "check your email."

It's not always easy, but this principle is critical for financial success. Disciplined prioritization involves allocating resources to investments before discretionary spending, engaging in uncomfortable financial conversations when necessary, and making difficult short-term sacrifices for long-term prosperity.

If you're serious about achieving financial independence, you need the discipline to consistently take action—especially when it's uncomfortable. "Pay the price today so you can pay any price tomorrow," Grant Cardone advises. This might mean studying when friends are partying, working weekends to build your business, or living below your means while your friends indulge freely.

Be disciplined about pursuing what benefits you in the long term, even when it's temporarily uncomfortable. Few people genuinely enjoy every workout, but disciplined individuals exercise consistently because they value the cumulative benefits over momentary comfort. For me, I keep my vision clear by looking in the mirror every day—checking to see if my abs are shy and hiding. If they are, I know I need to push harder. And if I can see my four-pack, then I'd better bring sexy back too—and work out even harder.

Discipline Area #2: Master Impulse Control Discipline

Here's the discipline secret nobody talks about: **willpower is overrated.**

Research shows you can only resist temptation about 6-7 times before giving in. So why would you rely on willpower when no one can rely on willpower alone forever? That's why the smarter move is to eliminate temptations, making it impossible to give in when your willpower is low.

Don't want to eat junk food? Don't buy junk food. The most effective strategy isn't willpower at the moment of craving, but rather the discipline to not bring unhealthy options into your home in the first place. Make temptation impossible by eliminating access—you can't go into the snack pantry at midnight when it's not there. Delete your ex's number so you can't call them when you're tempted. But if you have it memorized, well, you'd better hope your number is blocked!

Apply this to financial temptations. Unsubscribe from retail emails that trigger impulse purchases. Avoid browsing online stores when bored. Remove saved payment information from shopping sites to create barriers to impulsive spending.

Make it impossible to fail, rather than relying on superhuman self-control.

Discipline Area #3: Delayed Gratification (The Marshmallow Test for Adults)

Work first, then play. Earn first, then spend. Invest first, then enjoy. This isn't about avoiding celebration of genuine milestones—those deserve recognition. Instead, it's about the dangerous pattern of prioritizing enjoyment over work (or never do the work).

My son, Max, has a routine: shoes in the designated spot, backpack upstairs, lunch box by the sink, wash hands, change clothes, homework, and cleanup—*then* TV time. We created a visual checklist with pictures he drew himself, complete with flip cards he can turn as he completes each task.

The kid is six and already more disciplined than most adults I know.

The discipline of delayed gratification extends beyond daily routines to major financial decisions. If purchasing something requires your complete paycheck while still living on your mom's account, that means you can't truly afford it. Don't spend your entire paycheck on luxury items you can barely afford. Obviously, if you earn millions, different rules apply. Don't be that person with a Louis Vuitton purse or a Rolex watch, while driving a Honda and living in a house with no furniture.

"It's not your salary that makes you rich, it's your spending habits."

—*Charles A. Jaffe.*

The fundamental principle remains: save and invest first, then enjoy luxuries from allocated funds. The discipline to delay small gratifications that most people pursue (excessive entertainment, status purchases, lifestyle inflation) allows you to achieve bigger goals and financial freedom earlier than most.

The Discipline Compound Effect

Here's the beautiful thing about discipline: it compounds. Each small act of self-control makes the next one easier. Each completed task builds momentum for the next. Each "I did what I said I would do" moment strengthens your self-trust.

And self-trust? That's the foundation of confidence, which is the foundation of success, which is the foundation of wealth.

Your Discipline Upgrade Plan

Pick ONE area to be disciplined about:

- **Prioritization**: Do your hardest task before checking email
- **Impulse Control**: Remove one temptation from your environment
- **Delayed Gratification**: Earn your reward before taking it

Start small. Build momentum. Watch your entire life start organizing itself around your new standards.

Because when you master yourself, you can master anything.

Principle 4: **The Discipline Advantage**

Build unshakable discipline in prioritization, impulse control, and delayed gratification. These fundamental practices create both immediate effectiveness and long-term prosperity.

◉ Teach & Thrive

Here are some ways to build discipline in your children:

1. **Work-Before-Play Protocol:** Create visual "First → Then" charts showing required tasks before rewards. For younger children, use photos of them completing each step. Make the sequence explicit: homework → cleanup → skill practice → TV time. This trains automatic work-before-pleasure patterns.

2. **Environment Engineering:** Teach children to design their environment for success rather than testing willpower. For example, help them identify distractions during homework time and create systems to eliminate them—gathering materials beforehand and setting up a designated workspace. Don't stock unhealthy food. Don't set them up for failure by placing temptation in their path. Help them avoid environments that introduce destructive behaviors.

3. **The "Do It Anyway" Mindset:** Explain that life includes tasks we must do regardless of feelings. Provide examples: brushing teeth when tired, doing homework when you want to play. Frame it as building "discipline muscles" that make everything else easier. This plants the fundamental understanding that feelings don't control actions.

4. **Delayed Gratification Connection:** Utilize clear visual tools that show future benefits. To save money, use transparent jars with pictures of the desired items. For longer-term goals, create progress trackers where children color segments as they advance. This helps children naturally connect hard work today with rewards tomorrow.

5. **Hard-Work-First Connection Training:** Train children to understand that doing hard work first makes the rest easier. For example: I told Max, "Finish homework, clean up, and shower—then you'll have two hours to play uninterrupted. Play first, you'll have to stop your fun later and do work when you're tired." Max has already grasped this principle. Sometimes he proudly announces, "Luckily I already did homework and showered, otherwise I'd have to do it now!" Principle 31 will deepen this understanding to life-scale: work hard when you're young so you can enjoy freedom when you're older.

Remember: You're building their "discipline muscle" early so they can lift heavier life challenges later.

PRINCIPLE 5

Be Batman

*"The future belongs to those who believe
in the beauty of their dreams."*

—Eleanor Roosevelt

"I want to be Batman!" declared my six-year-old son Max while considering Halloween costumes. A moment later: "I want to be a skeleton too."

I don't understand why people choose to portray something ugly or dead when they could embody something beautiful or powerful. In life, we become what we envision ourselves to be. Halloween isn't just one night of pretend—it's a metaphor for identity selection.

"Why would you want to be a skeleton when you can be Batman?" I asked him. "This is your chance to become something AMAZING for a night. Batman is rich with incredible tools and abilities. A skeleton is dried up, lifeless, poor, and powerless. Which sounds better?"

"Batman!" he decided. And when asked about his superpower that year, he confidently announced: "I'm rich!" (movie reference)

This moment taught me everything about dream cultivation.

The Blank Canvas Principle

Every child starts as a blank canvas. Society, experiences, and random people all leave their marks. Some kids become masterpieces. Others... Well, let's just say not every canvas gets the Mona Lisa treatment.

As parents, we have a choice: deliberately guide our children's development, or let random people with questionable artistic skills splash paint wherever they want.

The Programming Reality

Here's the uncomfortable truth: something or someone WILL influence your children's desires and ambitions. If not you, then who? Their peers with limited life experience? Social media and news with their own agenda? Random environmental factors?

Some do transcend their environments and change their destinies. I'm not suggesting that children from challenging backgrounds can't achieve greatness—many certainly have. My point is that intentional guidance dramatically increases the chance of success. By deliberately shaping and directing our children's aspirations, we significantly increase their chances of success.

You might think, "But shouldn't kids choose their own paths?"

Okay. Fair question. However, they will still be influenced anyway. The question is: why not you?

Accidental Dream Programming

My brother's journey illustrates this principle perfectly. Our parents' friends constantly discussed their children becoming doctors. These conversations categorized physicians as prestigious, well-compensated heroes who save lives while achieving financial success. This powerful combination of purpose and prosperity became the "why" that motivated my brother throughout his education. The seed was planted through consistent exposure, whether intentionally or not.

My brother absorbed this programming and committed to a career in medicine in middle school. And yes, he maintained straight A's throughout his entire academic career because he had a clear target.

As for me, if you recall, I was programmed with the magical $100,000 number, which was a tremendous amount in my young mind.

Was this accidental genius or an intentional strategy? Looking back, it was unplanned programming. The goal was way too small, but that wasn't the point. I wish I were guided to 10X it. I was already much older when I realized it was a tiny goal. Since then, I have adjusted my goal.

Strategic Dream Implantation

What if we were *more* intentional about this programming?

Instead of hoping our children stumble into great dreams, what if we strategically expose them to extraordinary possibilities?

Give your children expansive goals, then multiply by ten. When Max said he wanted to be a millionaire, we said, "You can be a billionaire." And when he mentioned he likes building things, we said, "You could design and build incredible structures when you grow up!" We feed the dream instead of shrinking it down to a "realistic" size. It's about encouraging your kids not just to dream, but to choose to embody greatness rather than settle for something lesser. You're planting the seed that we all get to choose who we step into, even if just for a moment. Sometimes, even one moment is enough to set a belief for a lifetime.

The Vision-Action Connection

Dreams create vision. Vision creates focus. Focus creates action. Action creates results.

Without big dreams, children default to small thinking. They aim for "good enough" jobs, "decent" lifestyles, and "comfortable" futures. There's nothing wrong with comfort—but there's everything right with excellence.

What we feed our children's minds becomes their reality. Children are truly blank canvases, and we have the privilege of helping them visualize the image **they can paint for their future**. This isn't something we merely tell them once—it requires consistent reinforcement and environmental design.

Creating a vision of a compelling future with a clear purpose is essential for lasting success. Plant the right seeds, and you'll grow the right fruit.

"Don't judge each day by the harvest you reap but by the seeds that you plant."

—*Robert Louis Stevenson*

Your Dream Cultivation Assignment

Start planting bigger seeds in your children's minds:

- Talk about abundance instead of limitation
- Discuss what THEY love and steer them toward bigger versions
- Expose them to people who've achieved extraordinary things
- Ask "How can we..." instead of "We can't..."
- Share stories of people who started with less and achieved more

The Dreams-to-Reality Pipeline

Remember: you're not forcing career choices. You're expanding their sense of what's possible. A child who believes they can become a billionaire architect might "only" become a millionaire engineer—and that's still a massive win.

But a child who never dreams bigger than "getting a job" will likely get exactly that—just a J.O.B.

Plant ambitious seeds. Water them with encouragement.

Principle 5: **Strategic Dream Cultivation**

Plant ambitious seeds in young minds through deliberate exposure to possibilities. Guide children to envision expansive futures and develop compelling reasons that fuel persistent action.

◉ Teach & Thrive

Here are five powerful ways to cultivate big dreams in your children:

1. **Future Self Visualization:** Help your child create detailed visions of themselves at 25, 30, or 40. Where do they live? What have they created? How do they spend their days? What problems have they solved? Make it specific and exciting, not vague. Document these visions and revisit them regularly.

2. **Dream Board Creation:** Create a family "Dream Board" showcasing extraordinary achievements, innovations, and destinations. Include space for your child's specific dreams. Position it where they'll see it daily. This environmental cue consistently reinforces expansive thinking during their formative years.

3. **Success Story Immersion:** Watch age-appropriate documentaries about innovators and entrepreneurs together. Follow with family discussions: "What impressed you most? What would you do differently? What problems would you want to solve?" This builds entrepreneurial thinking patterns naturally.

4. **Dream Expansion Exercises:** When your child expresses interest in something, help them explore the biggest possible version of it. Like building? Maybe they'll design cities. Like animals? Perhaps

they'll create wildlife preserves. Like games? Maybe they'll build entertainment empires. Always expand, and never contract, their vision.

5. **Exposure to Accomplished People:** Introduce your children to high achievers through community events, lectures, or family connections. Prepare questions beforehand so your child can engage meaningfully. When success has a face and a story, it becomes attainable rather than abstract.

Goal: Raise children who see extraordinary achievement as normal and expected, not rare and lucky.

PRINCIPLE 6

High Price Tag

"I think; therefore I am."

—*René Descartes*

Would you rather be a Ferrari or a bus?

This question isn't about cars—it's about how you value yourself and how you expect to be treated by the world.

The fundamental truth is: Whatever you believe about yourself becomes your reality. Call yourself punctual, and you'll move mountains to arrive on time. Label yourself disorganized, and your environment will reflect that belief. Define yourself as health-conscious, and your food choices will naturally align with that identity. Identify yourself as valuable, and you'll become valuable.

Set a high price tag for yourself—then live up to it.

The Price Tag Psychology

Setting a high self-value creates three powerful advantages:

1. It pushes you to justify that value through your actions
2. It establishes clear guidelines for your integrity
3. It raises your standards for how others may treat you

Setting a high self-value puts you in a continuous state of self-improvement as you work to justify that value. With healthy self-respect, genuine confidence naturally develops. You'll instinctively rise to meet the expectations you've established for yourself.

Self-valuation also generates a protective sense of dignity. A person with healthy pride treats others well and behaves honorably—anything less would contradict their self-image. They avoid dishonorable actions not just because such behavior is wrong, but also because it would violate their sense of self. Even when no one is watching, their integrity remains intact because their standards are internal, not performative.

*"The soul becomes dyed
with the color of its thoughts."*

—*Marcus Aurelius, the Roman emperor and philosopher.*

Setting a high price tag for yourself creates natural protection against poor treatment. When you truly value yourself, you automatically reject substandard behavior from others in any relationship. You establish clear boundaries for acceptable treatment because you understand your worth. I want my kids to truly grasp this principle. It's not just about the people they encounter—it's about the relationships that can alter their life's trajectory, like friendships and a lifelong partner.

My Mother's Million-Dollar Lesson

This was one of my mother's most impactful teachings. When boys started showing interest in my teenage years, she pulled me aside with advice that shaped my entire relationship with self-worth.

"You must value yourself and set a high price for yourself," she said in her direct, no-nonsense way, which roughly translates to: "If you don't value yourself, others won't. Not everyone deserves access to you without qualification."

The Christmas Watch Incident

One Christmas, a street-smart boy secretly gave me a gift—a watch. When my mother discovered it, she instructed me to return it immediately.

"I don't need gifts from boys," she explained. "Your grandmother taught me never to accept flowers or gifts from men unless they've earned that privilege. They have to be LUCKY enough for you to accept their gifts. You're too valuable to accept presents from just anyone."

This might sound arrogant, but I understood the deeper principle. Some people use material gifts to create feelings of obligation or exploit vulnerabilities. When you don't have much, modest offerings can seem impressive and create compromising situations.

The issue wasn't the gift's value. The problem was the principle: accepting gifts creates reciprocal obligations, so you should be selective about whose gifts deserve acceptance.

Think about it: You wouldn't accept an engagement ring from just any guy, right? The principle scales. Accepting inevitably creates a reciprocal obligation. Shouldn't the giver consider himself fortunate that you would accept and return something of genuine value—your attention, time, or consideration? Being selective about whose gifts you accept is prudent self-protection.

In case you were curious about the watch, it was a Timex worth about twenty bucks or less at that time—still in some box somewhere in my mother's attic as a reminder of this valuable lesson. I'm opening the bidding at one million dollars. Do I hear one million? Who'll give me two?

The Armor of Self-Worth

This advice profoundly shaped my confidence and became my armor as I entered the dating world. I learned I didn't NEED anything from anyone, and that I couldn't be bought with gifts. (I did accept flowers occasionally—they die anyway and can't be returned, so minimal obligation created!)

The price tag you set for yourself directly influences your self-confidence, decision-making, and ability to maintain boundaries. When you genuinely value yourself, you naturally:

- Make better choices about relationships
- Maintain higher standards in all areas
- Refuse to accept substandard treatment
- Invest in your continued development
- Present yourself with pride and care

Your High-Value Upgrade Plan

Start treating yourself like the premium product you are. Remember to R.A.I.S.E.

- **Relationships:** Only accept treatment that honors your values
- **Appearance:** Present your best self, impeccably (this is SELF-RESPECT, not vanity)
- **Investment:** Continuously upgrade your knowledge, skills, and capabilities

- **Standards**: Hold yourself to expectations that justify your price tag
- **Environment**: Create spaces that reflect your worth

Remember: you can't price yourself like a Ferrari and perform like a Honda. The price tag must be backed by substance, effort, and continuous improvement.

> **But here's the secret: the higher you price yourself, the more motivated you become to justify that value.**

It's a beautiful upward spiral where self-worth drives self-improvement, which in turn validates self-worth, inspiring even more improvement.

Principle 6: **The Self-Worth Principle**

Set a premium price tag for yourself. Your personal valuation determines both how you treat yourself and how others treat you.

◉ Teach & Thrive

Here are five ways to help your children develop healthy self-valuation:

1. **Praise Vocabulary:** Replace generic praise ("good job") with specific worth acknowledgments: "You should be proud of yourself," "Your effort made a real difference," "That required courage." This builds internal vocabulary, connecting actions to identity rather than seeking external validation.

2. **Boundary Training:** Teach children to recognize and respond to boundary violations through role-playing. Practice phrases like "I'm not comfortable with that," "That doesn't work for me," or "I need you to stop." Start with simple scenarios before progressing to complex social situations. Teach children to stand up for themselves when someone says something negative or physically disrespects their boundaries. This builds verbal boundary enforcement skills that last a lifetime.

3. **Personal Standards Framework:** Help children develop decision-making based on personal values rather than external pressure. When facing choices, guide them through the question: "Does this align with who you are?" "Would someone who respects themselves choose this?" This teaches children to make decisions based on their own values instead of reacting to peer pressure, using their self-worth as a guide. For younger children, use simpler language: "Would good

people do this?" "Would rich people do this?" "Would someone clean and organized do this?"

4. **Self-Care:** Establish daily practices that reinforce worth through action: proper grooming, healthy eating, skill development, and rest. Frame these as "honoring your value" rather than chores. For younger children, create a "taking care of my valuable self" routine with specific steps.

5. **Selective Association Practice:** Help children thoughtfully choose affiliations rather than accepting whoever's available. Discuss friendship qualities before social situations arise. Create a "good qualities" list. Ask about friends' character traits regularly. This teaches children to choose friends based on character, not just convenience.

Goal: Raise confident children who know their worth, expect respectful treatment, and never settle for less than they deserve.

PRINCIPLE 7

Be Delusionally Confident

*"Whether you think you can
or you think you can't—you're right."*

—Henry Ford

You are what you believe about yourself. And if you're going to believe something, why not make it *amazing*?

Your self-perception influences every aspect of your life. Developing unshakable confidence creates a shield against negative talk and distraction from both internal and external sources.

It's perfectly okay—encouraged, even—to be a little "delusionally confident." Healthy high self-esteem isn't arrogance; it's survival gear for a world that will try to convince you you're not enough, don't deserve success, and should settle for mediocrity.

But here's the catch: you can't fake it till you make it forever.

Feeding Your Confidence Through Competence

The real key is this—real confidence must be backed by real results. You can't tag yourself with a Ferrari price while delivering Honda performance.

Without substance and evidence to justify your high self-worth, even the most optimistic self-belief eventually deflates.

True confidence needs to be fed. You build it through **S.T.A.C.K.E.R.**

- **Stack accomplishments** (even small wins)
- **Train and develop real skills** (not just positive thoughts)
- **Assess and increase self-awareness**
- **Cultivate a positive self-image** by looking your best (feeling good physically affects everything else)
- **Keep promises to yourself** (self-trust builds confidence)
- **Eliminate & avoid negative self-talk**
- **Remain committed to learning** (competence creates confidence)

Whatever you tell yourself consistently becomes your truth. When you truly believe something, it becomes your reality. Therefore, it's crucial to ensure your self-talk is constructive and empowering.

The Confidence Trinity

Let's clarify what we're building here, because people use these terms interchangeably when they're actually different:

- **Self-Confidence:** How much you TRUST yourself and your abilities. It's a positive belief that you can accomplish what you wish to do. Self-confidence differs from self-esteem, which is an evaluation of one's worth.
- **Self-Esteem:** How much you VALUE and LIKE yourself. It's based on our opinions and beliefs about ourselves.
- **Self-Image:** How you SEE yourself (and think others see you). Your mental picture of yourself, including how you believe others see you. Feeling good about your appearance and presentation is a crucial component of a healthy self-perception.

All three need to work together like a three-legged stool. Wobbly on any leg, and the whole thing topples.

A negative self-image often contributes to low self-esteem, while a positive self-image increases high self-esteem. Maintaining a positive self-image and building "undeflatable" self-confidence naturally produces healthy self-esteem.

Let me be frank and spell it out. Self-image refers to how you perceive and present yourself. If you show up looking messy, you'll feel messy and believe that you're less attractive. When that happens, you naturally start to value yourself less, slap a lower price tag on your worth, and your energy drops. That cycle leads to lower self-esteem, weaker self-confidence, and fewer wins in life. It's not just about putting on a nice shirt; it's about telling yourself that you are worth the effort and that you are valuable. So present yourself as if you're worth top dollar—not like you're on the clearance rack at a thrift store. That's the high-price-tag hack. You see, the cycle works both ways—it starts on the outside and builds up on the inside, and the inner confidence then shows up in how you present yourself. Each one fuels the other.

Enhance your self-image by consistently presenting your best self—maintaining physical health, dressing appropriately, and carrying yourself with good posture. When you look good, you feel good, which naturally improves self-image. This isn't about expensive clothes or what other people think of you—it's about self-respect and personal standards. Looking polished and appropriate shows respect for the venue, the occasion, those around you, and most importantly, yourself.

The Confidence Construction System

Level 1: Physical Foundation

When you look good, you feel good. This isn't vanity—it's psychology. Put effort into your appearance, maintain good posture, and dress appropriately for situations. When you respect yourself enough to present well, others respond differently, and you carry yourself differently.

My taekwondo-trained son learned this early: "Loving yourself means feeding your body healthy food and feeding your head good things." Six years old and already wiser than most adults!

Level 2: Competence Building

Confidence without competence is just delusion. But competence without confidence is wasted potential. You need both.

Fuel your confidence by acquiring valuable skills and accumulating meaningful accomplishments. Your capabilities, talents, and achievements provide genuine confidence with real substance. So, keep sharpening them continually, never stop learning, and continuously develop new abilities. That's how you become increasingly more well-rounded and naturally boost your confidence. Consequently, you'll be worth the price tag you've assigned yourself.

Level 3: Internal Narrative

Whatever you tell yourself repeatedly becomes your truth. When you truly believe something, it becomes a part of your reality. If you consistently think "I'm not good at this," "I can't do this," "I'm so messy," or "I'm not good enough," your subconscious mind starts believing. That's why it's crucial to ensure your self-talk is constructive and empowering.

Flip the script. "I'm learning this." "I can do it." "I'm becoming successful." "I'm organized." "I deserve good things." Say it enough, and your brain starts finding evidence to support these beliefs instead of contradicting them.

The Confidence-Reality Loop

The lesson here is the trifecta of confidence-building: looking your best, stacking accomplishments, and gaining skills that earn serious money. It all begins with setting a high price tag and consistently working to justify that value. Continue to develop your worth and elevate your standards. As Bruce Lee put it, "As you think, so shall you become." The story you tell yourself is where it all begins—and the value you place on yourself is what the world will reflect to you.

It's a positive feedback loop that keeps building momentum.

My Kids' Confidence Training Program

I praise my children for every positive action and small accomplishment. They get to make their own choices (from approved options), try new things without pressure, and learn that mistakes are data, not disasters.

Max takes taekwondo for discipline and confidence. He has had piano recitals to practice performing in front of an audience. Both kids help with cooking, cleaning, and contributing to the household, as productivity builds self-worth.

Looking nice when we go out? Non-negotiable. Not because appearance is everything, but because self-care is a form of self-respect, and self-respect fuels confidence.

Your Confidence Upgrade Protocol

1. **Look your best** consistently (respect yourself through presentation)
2. **Stack wins daily** (even tiny accomplishments count)
3. **Learn something new** regularly (competence creates confidence)
4. **Keep promises to yourself** (self-trust is confidence fuel)

5. **Upgrade your self-talk** (you're listening to yourself all day)

Be delusionally confident in your potential, then make that delusion your reality.

> **Here is the open secret formula that creates unshakable confidence: Look your best + Stack accomplishments/skills + Make serious money = Genuine confidence that can weather any storm.**

Principle 7: **The Confidence Formula**

Systematically build genuine confidence through skill development, achievement accumulation, and positive self-image cultivation. External confidence stems from internal belief, backed by substantive capability.

◎ Teach & Thrive

Here are five ways to build authentic confidence in your children:

1. **Competence-Based Praise System:** Replace generic praise ("good job") with specific capability recognition: "You persisted when that was difficult," "You solved that problem creatively," "You helped someone who needed it." This builds confidence based on actual demonstrated abilities rather than empty encouragement.

2. **Challenge Calibration:** Design activities that are 70% achievable, 30% stretch. Too easy builds false confidence that collapses under real pressure. Too hard destroys confidence through repeated failure. When you play with your children or create a game/challenge for them, make it hard but not too hard, and let them win by design. Encourage the "How Can I" mindset: when they don't know how to do something, guide them to ask, "How can I?" instead of saying, "I can't, or I don't know how?"

3. **Performance Opportunity Progression:** Systematically increase your child's comfort with being seen and evaluated. Begin with family presentations, then progress to small groups, and finally to larger audiences. Prepare them with specific tools to manage their nerves. Each successful experience builds confidence for bigger challenges.

4. **Skill Documentation Portfolio & Sharing Wins:** Create moments where everyone takes turns sharing accomplishments. Create visual records of your child's developing capabilities. Photos of projects, videos of improvements, and certificates of achievements. This tangible evidence of growth becomes confidence fuel during moments of self-doubt. They can literally see their progress. For Example, Max is taking Taekwondo, and he gets a trophy for each belt level he moves up.

5. **Mistake Reframing as Learning:** Transform setbacks into confidence builders through consistent reframing. When things don't go as planned, guide them through the question: "What did you learn that makes you stronger?" "What part did you handle well?" "How does this prepare you for next time?" This builds resilience-based confidence rather than fragile success-dependent confidence

Goal: Raise children with unshakeable confidence based on genuine capability, continuous growth, and resilient self-trust.

Foundation to Cultivate the Seed

Building the Essential Mindset for Wealth

Principle 1: The First Step to Having Anything | *The Power of Wealth Conditioning*. Expose children to wealth and abundance early—you can't want what you don't know exists. Conditioning for wealth begins with seeing what's possible.

Principle 2: Lobsters From Maine | *The High Standards Advantage*. Set high standards for everything: experiences, relationships, and personal conduct. High standards create both protection against negativity and a sense of propulsion toward excellence.

Principle 3: Good Things Come to Those Who Appreciate | *The Appreciation Advantage*. Genuine appreciation creates a virtuous cycle of abundance. The more you appreciate, the more good things flow to you.

Principle 4: Build Discipline and Slap Your Lower Self | *The Discipline Advantage*. Master prioritization, impulse control, and delayed gratification. Discipline is the foundation that makes all other success possible.

Principle 5: Be Batman | *Strategic Dream Cultivation*. Plant ambitious dreams early through strategic exposure. Guide children to envision expansive futures and develop compelling motivations.

Principle 6: High Price Tag | *The Self-Worth Principle*. Set a premium value for yourself. Your self-worth determines how you treat yourself and how others treat you.

Principle 7: Be Delusionally Confident | *The Confidence Formula.*
Build authentic confidence through skill development, achievement
accumulation, and a positive self-image—back it up with real capability.

Fundamental Habits

PRINCIPLE 8

Good Habits Pay Off

> *"We are what we repeatedly do.*
> *Excellence, then, is not an act, but a habit."*
>
> —*Aristotle*

The Discipline-Habit Connection

Discipline is doing something you need to do even when you don't want to. Habit is doing something so automatically that you don't even think about it—like brushing your teeth or checking your phone 847 times a day. (Hey, no judgment here.)

The difference? Discipline requires constant willpower. Habit is on autopilot—once established, it operates with minimal conscious effort.

Discipline forces you to act against immediate desires—exercising when you'd rather watch television, saving money when you want to spend it. Habit operates automatically, requiring no conscious effort or internal deliberation. The person who brushes their teeth each morning doesn't debate the decision; they act.

The Power of Starting Strong

Beginning each day with an empowering routine saves time, creates early victories, and establishes positive momentum. Rise early without snoozing or scrolling. Begin with gratitude or a spiritual practice, prepare your physical space, exercise your body, center your mind, and find gratitude.

The snooze button represents a small but significant habit that undermines discipline. Some people delay getting out of bed for 30-60 minutes by repeatedly snoozing. If you truly need that additional rest, set your alarm for your actual rising time and enjoy uninterrupted sleep. Each unnecessary snooze subtly weakens your self-discipline muscle. If you snooze so much, you will create a habit of snoozing away your success, too.

Don't wait for the perfect conditions to start building better habits. Start with whatever time you have, wherever you are, with whatever energy remains. The key is consistency, not perfection.

Here's the truth that most people miss: your morning sets the trajectory for your entire day, and your daily habits ultimately determine the trajectory of your life. Combine intentional morning practices with systematic habit-building, and you've got the operating system that runs successful lives.

As Louise Hay said, "How you start your day determines how you live your day. How you live your day determines how you live your life."

The Father's Mirror Wisdom

When I was young, my father shared a simple yet profound practice that has shaped my mornings for decades: "Look in the mirror every morning, smile, and say it's going to be a good day."

This basic habit became the foundation for everything else. Starting each day by literally smiling at yourself creates an intentional moment of positivity before the world can throw chaos at you. This sets a positive tone for the day.

My complete morning routine now begins with this wisdom and builds from there:

1. The first thing that wakes me up is stretching like a cat—arms extended, legs elongated, back gently arched. Then comes prayer and affirmations. I rise, approach the mirror, smile at my reflection, and declare, "It's going to be a great day!" as I get ready.

2. I've incorporated a quick facial massage using a roller after applying moisturizer—a small self-care ritual that takes minimal additional time yet yields noticeable benefits. Following this, I enjoy warm lemon water, begin my workout, and meditate. These sequential victories create powerful momentum before my workday even begins.

3. I then review my priorities and plan my approach, tackling my most challenging tasks first while my energy remains strongest.

Teaching Children the Daily Success Framework

Sometimes my children wake up whining or cranky. I consistently remind them: "Always start the morning happily and you'll have a happy day. First, say 'Good morning. I love you, Mama. I love you, Daddy. I'm happy.' Then tell me what you need."

We discuss our daily plan together: "Let's brush our teeth and get ready, then go downstairs for breakfast. If you're quick, you can play for a bit before we visit the park. After the park, we'll have lunch at a restaurant, then come home to relax and watch something. Later, you can visit grandma."

This daily planning process benefits everyone regardless of age, though its impact on adult productivity and achievement can be profound. Beginning each day with intention rather than reaction fundamentally alters your results.

The Morning-to-Evening Success Loop

Your morning routine creates momentum, your daily habits maintain it, and your evening preparation sets the stage for tomorrow's success. This isn't just about productivity—it's about designing a life that naturally moves you towards your biggest goals.

Planning your day reduces decision fatigue and ensures essential tasks get attention when your energy is at its highest. Whether you're eight years old, planning your after-school activities, or forty-eight, planning your business priorities, intentional day design beats reactive scrambling every time.

The Science of Habit Formation

The quality of your life directly correlates with the standards you maintain and the habits you've installed. The foundation built early determines your long-term trajectory. Commit to daily improvement through systematically installing positive habits while eliminating negative ones.

Negative habits form effortlessly and often unconsciously. But positive habits require deliberate effort and persistence. Popular belief is that it takes 21 days to form a habit, but that's a myth—that's about as scientific as saying chocolate is a vegetable because cocoa beans grow on trees. Research indicates that it takes the average person approximately 66 days to fully incorporate a new behavior; this timeline varies based on the complexity, personal motivation, and consistency of practice.

Breaking existing poor habits while installing beneficial replacements requires significantly more energy than building fresh habits on a clean foundation. This reality makes early habit formation incredibly valuable, particularly for children whose neural pathways remain highly adaptable.

So start them YOUNG! Daily implementation is a critical factor in successfully installing a habit.

My Three-Pillar Framework for Wealth-Building Habits

Through years of observing successful people and analyzing my own wealth-building journey, I've discovered that every powerful habit serves your financial future through one of three fundamental mechanisms. This "PHI" framework has become my personal filter for evaluating which habits deserve precious time and energy:

1. PREVENT unnecessary LOSSES and setbacks
2. Helps you GAIN valuable resources or opportunities
3. IMPROVE toward desired outcomes

I use this simple framework as my decision-making tool when evaluating any potential habit. I ask myself: Does this behavior protect what I have, help me acquire more, or improve my systems for achieving my goals? If a habit doesn't clearly serve one of these purposes, it doesn't deserve space in my carefully designed life.

Through personal experience, I've learned that with sufficient repetition over the years, beneficial habits become ingrained in your system, your muscle memory, and your very identity. They transform from conscious effort into automatic advantage. This integration process works most effectively when started at a young age, which is why installing these patterns in your children represents one of your most important parenting responsibilities.

The organizational habits I'll share next perfectly demonstrate this framework in action.

The Daily Cost of Disorganization

My aunt provides a sobering example of how poor organizational habits compound into significant life penalties. Almost every morning, I witness the same frustrating ritual: she spends ten to fifteen minutes frantically searching for misplaced keys.

The scene unfolds predictably—purse contents scattered across counters, coat pockets frantically checked, couch cushions lifted in desperation. Her face shows increasing stress as departure time approaches and keys remain missing. The physical search represents only the visible cost; the mental energy drain and morning stress affect her decision-making capacity for hours afterward.

Calculate the mathematics: fifteen minutes daily equals over ninety hours annually spent on completely avoidable searching. Those same ninety hours could fund substantial financial education, skill development, or income-generating activities. Multiply this pattern across multiple misplaced items and inefficient processes, and disorganization literally costs years of productive potential.

More critically, organizational chaos creates mental chaos, undermining strategic thinking and sound financial decision-making. When your physical environment is constantly disorderly, your mind struggles to maintain the clarity required for wealth-building activities, such as investment analysis, business planning, or systematic saving.

Essential Daily Habit Categories That Matter

Category 1: Organizational Excellence

Practice organizational habits by establishing designated homes for your belongings, so that even during chaotic periods, you can locate items through systematic thinking rather than frantic searching.

Always return your phone, keys, and wallet to designated locations immediately after use. This eliminates the frustration and time waste of searching for misplaced essentials. Always scan your surroundings before departing any location to prevent leaving items behind—this small habit can save you countless frustrations and lost time.

My aunt's daily hunt for her keys illustrates the cumulative cost of disorganization. Developing logical systems for item placement means that even when you occasionally forget where something is, you can logically deduce its location.

I was fortunate to receive organizational training during childhood, instilling systems thinking that has served me throughout my wealth-building journey. Even during moments of chaos or distraction, I can revert to logical placement patterns that prevent loss of time or resources.

Organization represents the bedrock habit that supports all wealth-building activities. This sounds deceptively simple, yet the difference between organized and disorganized people often determines the difference between financial success and persistent struggle.

Certain habits become nearly impossible to change in adulthood, and organizational systems represent a critical example. Many people remain unaware of their destructive organizational patterns until those patterns have cost them years, thousands of dollars, and countless opportunities.

The profound truth about organization is that it's more than efficiency: when your house is clean and organized, it becomes a sanctuary. There's something almost magical about walking into a well-ordered space—you can actually breathe deeper, your shoulders relax, and you feel like you're living in luxury rather than chaos. It's the difference between coming home to a spa-like retreat versus walking into a disaster zone that immediately drains your energy.

Conversely, chaos in your physical environment creates chaos in your mental environment. When you're surrounded by clutter and disorganization, even simple decisions feel overwhelming, and you certainly can't think clearly about important financial choices when your surroundings constantly stress you.

> Here is the connection: organization extends far beyond organizing physical things to encompassing your schedule, projects, documents, bookkeeping, finances, and life.

Category 2: Continuous Learning and Improving

Make learning and improvement a daily habit. Making self-improvement addictive creates one of the most powerful wealth-building habits possible. The more you feed your mind valuable information, the more you crave intellectual growth. The more you develop yourself, the more addictive self-improvement becomes. Consistently improving yourself fills available time with productive activity, naturally eliminating space for negative or wasteful behaviors.

Category 3: Morning Routine as Success Programming

Starting each day with intentional actions rather than reactive responses programs your brain for proactive decision-making. This mental state influences every subsequent choice, from spending decisions to investment opportunities to career advancement actions.

These practices create ripple effects throughout your financial life, compounding benefits in ways that become visible only over extended periods. The person who consistently implements beneficial habits will always outperform someone with superior natural talent but poor habits and systems.

Category 4: Self-Care Standards

Self-care represents self-respect. Maintaining cleanliness and presenting yourself appropriately are essential components of your personal brand and image, directly affecting your self-confidence and how others perceive you.

Why Habits Create Wealth

Your daily habits directly determine your financial destiny. The small actions you repeat consistently—checking your budget, saving before spending, learning new skills—compound over time into extraordinary results. Conversely, poor habits create the opposite effect, slowly but relentlessly undermining financial progress.

Consider this: someone who automatically saves 20% of every paycheck will accumulate wealth, while someone who habitually spends everything will perpetually struggle. The difference isn't income level—it's the power of installed systems that operate without conscious effort.

As Aristotle observed, "Good habits formed at youth make all the difference." Installing good habits during childhood creates neural pathways that support wealth accumulation throughout life.

New Habit Installation Formula

Here's the game-changer: the easiest way to build a new habit is to attach it to something you already do. It's called "habit stacking". I think it's more like "habit stringing": an existing habit helps pull the new one.

The formula is simple: **After [THING YOU ALREADY DO], I will [NEW THING].**

Your brain already has superhighways built for your existing habits. By stringing a new habit to one of these automatic behaviors, you're basically piggybacking on those neural pathways that are already strong. And it's the reason my facial-rolling routine actually happens, instead of sitting in a drawer with good intentions.

My Facial Roller Victory

I wanted to incorporate facial exercises because nobody wants a saggy face or double chin, right? The roller stimulates blood circulation, and tones facial muscles—but only if you actually use it consistently. (Shocker, I know.)

Here's how I made it stick: **After I put on my face moisturizer, I immediately do my facial rolling routine.** I've found that it's the easiest and best time to do it. The moisturizer is my trigger. The rolling happens automatically. I've managed to squeeze in a facial rolling routine by attaching it to something I already do every morning. The entire thing takes maybe 60 seconds to 3 minutes. I figure if water can reshape stones over time, I just need to consistently do it every day.

The key? Pick ONE new habit. Attach it to one existing habit. Make it so easy you'd feel silly not doing it.

The trigger is built into your routine. One habit alerts the next. No separate reminder is needed. No decision fatigue. No willpower battles. Just automatic progress toward your goals.

Your Habit Building Challenge

What new habits do you want to establish?

For example:

- After I stretch, I will say my affirmation and gratitude
- After I drink my morning cup of warm water, I take my vitamins
- After the kids sleep, I read a couple of chapters

The Meta-Habit: Building Habit-Building Habits

Develop a meta-habit—the habit of continuously building positive habits. Make building good habits your biggest **obsession.** Good habits generate exponential returns through saved time, conserved resources, and increased productivity.

The most successful people aren't necessarily the smartest—they're the ones who've designed their daily patterns to automatically generate progress toward their goals.

Every financially successful person I know shares this trait: they've mastered the art of beneficial habits. Understanding this distinction will change how you approach both your success and your children's future prosperity.

Principle 8: **The Habit Installation Framework**

Systematically identify and install positive automatic behaviors. Make habit-building itself a habit, knowing that your daily patterns ultimately determine your destination.

◎ Teach & Thrive

Here are powerful methods to develop comprehensive daily success systems in your children:

1. **Morning Victory Routine:** Transform how children start each day by building positive momentum. Create a visual "Morning Champion" routine: includes wake-up stretching, positive mirror affirmation (smile and say, "Today will be great!"), basic hygiene, a healthy breakfast, and one organizational task. Time their improvements and celebrate consistency streaks. For younger children, create a song or chant; for older children, let them design their own sequence. This helps build the understanding that intentional mornings lead to intentional days.

2. **Habit Installation Experiment:** Make habit-building exciting through systematic experimentation. Create a "Habit Scientist" approach where children identify one slight improvement to test for a week and then evaluate the results. Use visual tracking appropriate to age—sticker charts for little ones, digital apps for teens. Focus on making tiny changes: making your bed, putting belongings in designated spots, or reading for 10 minutes daily. This builds the crucial meta-skill of intentional pattern creation.

3. **Day Architecture Training:** Teach children to plan their day intentionally. Help them identify their most important task, choose the best time to do it, and schedule activities around when they have the most energy. For younger children, use visual schedules with pictures and simple time concepts; for older children, introduce time-blocking and priority matrices. Review actual results against plans to build planning accuracy. This develops strategic thinking about time and energy management.

4. **Organization System Building:** Develop children's ability to create logical systems for their belongings and responsibilities. Create an "Everything Has a Home" system, where they designate specific locations for essential items and practice returning them immediately after use. Max follows a specific after-school sequence—backpack organized, lunch box cleaned, hands washed, clothes changed. Both of my kids are trained to put their shoes in the designated area.

5. **Evening Success Preparation:** Establish family practices for daily reflection and tomorrow's setup. Create "Day Review" conversations asking: "What went really well today?" "What could we improve tomorrow?" and "What's the plan for tomorrow?" Help children prepare for success by laying out clothes, organizing backpacks, and mentally rehearsing essential tasks. This builds the crucial habit of intentional preparation rather than morning scrambling.

Goal: Help your children build automatic success systems—the habits that will carry them to their dreams without constant willpower battles.

PRINCIPLE 9

Collect Rocks

*"The secret to getting ahead
is getting started."*

—*Mark Twain*

My brother and I were professional collectors as kids. Remember Pogs? We collected them and we'd trade constantly, always scheming to get better-condition pieces for our collections. We even started making our own by hammering bottle caps flat, basically becoming little entrepreneurs without realizing it.

Most parents think childhood collecting is just a cute form of playtime. They're missing something huge about the connection to accumulating assets. That collecting bug, when you let it run wild in the right direction, actually trains your brain for building wealth.

I collected everything: rocks with dazzling patterns, shells from the beach, and interesting bottles that seemed too special to throw away. My brother collected baseball cards and treated his collection like precious artifacts, organizing them in protective sleeves and constantly rearranging them by condition and value whenever he acquired new ones.

But the most critical thing we collected was money. We'd get those red envelopes from aunts and uncles during birthdays and holidays, and we treated them like treasure. We kept everything in a shoebox that became our personal bank vault. Every time we got a new envelope, we'd dump everything out and recount our fortune, like we were running our own financial empire.

Our "Massive" Fortune

Looking back, our wealth wasn't exactly impressive. We probably had less than $200 total, mostly wrinkled one-dollar bills that felt huge in our little hands. As we grew older, our savings increased to a few hundred dollars, eventually reaching close to $1,000, which felt like a fortune.

I still remember how those bills felt when I counted them. Heavy. Important. My fingers would actually get tired from handling each one, smoothing them out, organizing them by size. That shoebox felt like it contained our entire future. I genuinely thought we had so much money that counting it was exhausting work. What a great problem to have!

The Collection Psychology

Here's what I didn't realize at the time: collecting was programming my brain for wealth accumulation. The excitement of adding new items, organizing and reorganizing by value, trading up for better pieces—these weren't just childhood games. They were wealth-building behavior training.

Fast-forward to adulthood, and that same collecting mindset naturally transferred to my bank account, investment portfolio, and asset accumulation. What started with rocks and bottle caps evolved into rental properties and financial assets.

This foundation is gold when you start building real wealth. Adults who learned systematic collecting as children naturally approach buying assets with discipline and long-term thinking, whereas others have to force themselves to learn.

Why Collecting = Wealth Training

Collecting teaches fundamental W.E.A.L.T.H. principles:

- **Waiting (Patience):** Waiting for the right piece rather than settling
- **Evaluation:** Learning to assess quality and worth
- **Acquisition:** Actively seeking and obtaining valuable items
- **Logistics (Organization):** Systematically managing and displaying assets
- **Trading:** Exchanging lesser items for more valuable ones
- **Holding (Appreciation):** Understanding how value can increase over time

These aren't just hobby skills—they're investor skills.

From Rocks to Riches

This collecting mindset just naturally grew into adult money habits. Not because rocks are valuable, but because the BEHAVIOR of collecting, organizing, and systematically building something bigger is the foundation of all financial success. My bank account became another collection to build up, just like those childhood treasures. Real estate investments were like upgraded trading pods.

Remember the kid who spends hours organizing baseball cards? The child who's always trading up for better pieces? That same kid grew up becoming a professional sports card trader. My brother has sold some of his collectibles and made generous profits. He manages his card investment and continues trading as a side hobby.

The Monopoly Money Effect

Remember playing Monopoly as a kid? That thrill of accumulating properties, collecting rent, building your empire? Same psychological training, different medium.

Board games condition us to think in terms of:

- Asset acquisition
- Cash flow generation
- Strategic expansion
- Risk management
- Long-term wealth building

Then we grow up and... forget all these lessons in favor of spending everything we earn on stuff that depreciates.

My Kids' Collection Strategy

Max and Evelyn have multiple collections going: special rocks, coins, and small toys they've earned through our token system. But more importantly, they have savings jars with clear goals attached.

We created a trade-up system: five stars = one gold coin, two gold coins = $1. They're learning that smaller items can combine into something bigger, and bigger goals require patience and accumulation.

The Adult Collection Upgrade

As adults, we collect:

- Skills and knowledge
- Professional relationships

- Investment accounts
- Real estate properties
- Income streams
- Positive experiences

The psychology remains the same: identify valuable items, systematically acquire them, organize and optimize your collection, and trade up when opportunities arise.

Your Collection Assignment

If you're not naturally a collector, start small:

- Collect dollar bills in a jar (or savings account)
- Collect business cards from interesting people
- Collect screenshots of inspiring achievements
- Collect small investments in index funds
- Collect compliments and positive feedback

The medium doesn't matter. What matters is training your brain to systematically acquire and organize valuable items instead of randomly consuming and discarding it.

Principle 9: **The Acquisition Mindset**

The collecting mindset from childhood naturally grows into wealth-building behavior, teaching patience, organization, and smart accumulation that becomes the foundation for lifelong financial success.

◎ Teach & Thrive

Here are five ways to develop the acquisition mindset in your children:

1. **Meaningful Collection Development:** Help your child start a collection aligned with their interests—such as coins, interesting rocks, sports cards, or digital items for older children. Create a comprehensive organization system with proper storage and cataloging methods. This teaches the complete acquisition cycle: selection, acquisition, organization, maintenance, and strategic upgrading.

2. **Value Recognition Training:** Help your child pick collections based on what genuinely excites them—coins from different countries, sports cards, geodes, or favorite book series. Genuine interest keeps them engaged in the long term and teaches the patience essential for wealth building. It has to be their passion, not yours. Max has started to collect coins and Batman Lego sets

3. **Set up Trading and Upgrade Systems:** Create a system like our star-to-coin exchange (5 stars = one gold coin, two gold coins = $1). Encourage trading with friends to get better pieces. This teaches negotiation, evaluating opportunities, and the upgrade mentality that drives wealth building.

4. **Connect Collecting to Real Value:** Show them how being selective and patient can result in collections that actually grow in value over time. This plants early seeds for understanding how investments work.

5. **Digital-Physical Bridge Building:** For older children, create connections between physical collections and digital asset concepts. Help them understand how collection principles transfer to modern investment vehicles. A baseball card collection might evolve into fractional stock ownership in sports companies, demonstrating how childhood behaviors develop into sophisticated adult strategies.

Goal: Install the collector's psychology that naturally leads to systematic asset accumulation and wealth building.

Build a Tent

*"It's not about your resources.
It's about your resourcefulness."*

—*Tony Robbins*

Why Resourceful Kids Become Rich Adults

Before they became millionaires, successful people all learned the same critical skill: how to make things work with whatever they had available—find a way. When you let your kids build things from scratch instead of handing them perfect solutions, you're training their brains for the exact thinking that creates wealth later in life. Kids who know how to be resourceful—who build, create, and solve problems with pure creativity—develop the thinking patterns that generate wealth.

When I was little, my cousins and I were part of a youth group at our church that held this annual camp event. But it wasn't your typical summer camp—it was a "neighborhood campout". Families in our neighborhood volunteered their front yards, and we'd have this massive tent-building competition. Eight teams got assigned spaces, and our mission was simple: build the best tent using only materials we could scavenge from our homes.

We gathered blankets, clothes, mats, sticks, wire, string, ropes—basically anything that could be repurposed into shelter architecture. Our engineering approach involved creating triangular supports connected by a horizontal beam, and then covering the entire structure with fabric.

Spoiler alert: our first attempt collapsed faster than a house of cards in a hurricane. But we learned, adapted, and eventually created a tent so secure it could probably survive a mild earthquake. (Okay, maybe not, but it lasted the whole weekend!). We got creative with ropes, tying them to light poles and nearby trees for extra support.

The Accidental Genius of Having Less

Growing up without an abundance of toys forced me to be creative. We made kites from scratch and held racing competitions. We crafted slingshots for target practice. We built elaborate Barbie houses in the backyard using sticks and string, complete with a five-inch "well" we dug and filled with water.

By age eight, I was hand-sewing doll clothes. By eleven, I was operating a professional sewing machine with confidence. This foundation led to altering my clothes and making all my Halloween costumes instead of buying them—a personal challenge I maintain to this day.

Why "Building from Nothing" Matters

This matters for building wealth because this constant "figure it out" mentality trains your brain to see solutions where others see problems.

Research confirms what our parents' generation knew instinctively: **children with fewer toys develop greater creativity and resourcefulness.** When you can't just buy the solution, you learn to CREATE the solution.

This translates directly to financial success through:

- **Innovation skills** (finding new ways to solve problems)
- **Resource optimization** (making the most of what you have)
- **Opportunity recognition** (seeing possibilities others miss)
- **Cost consciousness** (knowing when to buy vs. build)

I still use this approach today. For my wedding, I didn't want to budget for a giant, expensive cake that would take days to finish and probably taste terrible under all that decorative icing. Instead, I figured out a creative solution: I ordered three simple, delicious cakes in different sizes from a local grocery store that made amazing, moist cakes without excessive sweetness.

My sister stacked them and added fresh flowers at the corners of each layer. It looked beautiful, tasted incredible, and cost a fraction of what a traditional wedding cake would have run us. I won't claim I invented the concept, but I'd never seen it done that way before. Years later, I started seeing people share this as a "wedding cake hack" online. Great minds think alike, right?

The "How Can I..." Mindset

The key is training your brain to automatically ask "HOW can I do this?" instead of "I can't do this because..."

- HOW can I create this experience on a budget?
- HOW can I solve this problem with existing resources?
- HOW can I make this work with what I have?
- HOW can I improve this process?

This thinking pattern becomes invaluable in business, investing, and wealth building. While others see obstacles, you see construction materials. This mindset directly translates to wealth building. Instead of thinking "I can't afford that," you start thinking "How can I create that?" Instead of waiting for perfect conditions, you figure out how to move forward with the resources you have. Instead of buying expensive solutions, you innovate cheaper, often better alternatives.

The kid who builds a fort out of couch cushions grows into the adult who launches a business from their garage.

Your Building Challenge

This week, identify one problem you've been throwing money at and engineer a creative solution instead. Maybe it's:

- Storage organization using items you already own
- Fixing broken items in your house before buying replacements
- Entertainment options that don't require spending
- Efficiency improvements using free tools
- Skill development through free resources

The goal isn't being cheap—it's developing the creative problem-solving muscle that generates wealth, rather than just spending it.

From Tent Building to Empire Building

Every successful entrepreneur is essentially a tent builder—taking limited resources and creating something valuable through creativity, persistence, and strategic thinking.

Start building. Start creating. Start asking "how". Your future wealth might be hidden in today's creative solutions.

Principle 10: **The Resourcefulness Mindset**

Developing resourceful creativity in childhood—learning to build, create, and solve problems with available materials—trains the innovative thinking patterns. Cultivate the habit of creating solutions with available resources. Consistently ask "how" questions to develop the problem-solving creativity that underlies financial success.

◉ Teach & Thrive

Here are five ways to develop creative problem-solving in your children:

1. **Constraint-Based Challenges:** Create projects that have intentional limitations, such as "Create a toy using only recycling bin items" or "Build a fort without using furniture." These constraints force creative thinking within boundaries—mimicking real-world resource limitations. Document solutions in an "Innovation Wall" (take pictures and post/print) to build confidence in their problem-solving capabilities.

2. **Repair-Before-Replace Protocol:** Before replacing broken items, attempt to repair or repurpose them first. When something breaks, brainstorm potential solutions before considering replacement. This builds the fundamental wealth mindset that resources are valuable and problems are opportunities for creative solutions.

3. **Monthly Invention Challenges:** Host regular invention challenges where family members identify everyday problems using household materials. Focus on the process over perfection—the goal is to develop problem-identification and solution-creation habits. This fosters the

entrepreneurial mindset that generates wealth by solving valuable problems.

4. **Resource Maximization Games:** Create competitions to stretch resources further. The "$5 Challenge" is a game in which each family member creates the most interesting experience possible with $5. Or "Pantry Challenges" to make meals using only existing ingredients. These activities develop the mindset of maximizing available resources rather than defaulting to additional spending.

5. **Solution-Finding Training:** Look for daily family routines that can be streamlined or improved together. For example, with two kids, we used to have each parent handle one child getting in and out of the car from our respective sides. But we got distracted and forgot to close doors a few times, leaving them wide open in the parking lots. So we all discussed it as a family and decided both kids should use the passenger side only—my side. The bonus is that it makes it much easier for my husband to open and close my door as well. This makes it easier for them to be chivalrous, too. These minor process improvements teach kids to constantly look for better ways to do things, which later translates directly into business-optimization thinking. Plus, they learn that sound systems eliminate chaos.

Goal: Develop children who view problems as construction materials for creative solutions rather than obstacles that require expensive fixes.

PRINCIPLE 11

Don't Wait for the Eggs to Boil

> *"Lost time is never found again."*
>
> —Benjamin Franklin

I never schedule a specific time for laundry. You'll never hear me say, "I need to stay home this weekend to do laundry." That's because I treat laundry like a background process—start a load before cooking dinner and transfer it to the dryer when I get home from errands.

Efficiency is about doing the right things at the right time.

And definitely don't stand there watching water boil, as if you're hypnotized by the world's most boring magic show.

The Efficiency Revelation

While eggs boil, I unload the dishwasher, prep ingredients, or set the table. While the pan heats up, I gather supplies, grab plates, and mince garlic.

This isn't about becoming a productivity robot. It's about recognizing that waiting time is gift time—extra minutes the universe is handing you to accomplish something worthwhile. It does add up, and in the end, you'll have more time to allocate to something else or enjoy the leisure of nothing.

The Kids' Evening Routine Masterclass

Picture this: 4:00-7:00 p.m. with two small children who want to do EVERYTHING and never want the day to end. Required activities: dinner, bath, bedtime routine. Desired activities: outdoor play, TV time.

When they negotiate for extended TV time before dinner, I explain: "It's beautiful outside and still light. If you watch TV now, it'll be dark after dinner—no outdoor time. But if you play outside first, you can watch TV when it's dark anyway. You get BOTH activities instead of just one."

Mind = blown. (Theirs and mine, honestly.)

The Errand Efficiency Test

How many times have you driven across town to return one item, then the next day found yourself in that same area for something else? That first trip was a waste of money and time.

I batch errands geographically and temporally. If I need to go to three stores, I map the most efficient route. If something isn't urgent, it waits until I'm already in that area for something else.

That's a no-brainer, right? But I was surprised to see how many people were running errands every day, and then wondered why they didn't have time to exercise.

Time as Puzzle Pieces

Think of your daily activities as puzzle pieces that need to fit into a 24-hour frame. A strategic arrangement creates space for additional accomplishments or leisure time. Poor sequencing leaves gaps and creates stress.

Example: Some people claim they can't exercise because they're "too tired after work" or "it's too hot at midday." This isn't a time problem—it's a sequencing problem. Schedule workouts when energy is high and temperature is optimal, not when you're exhausted and miserable.

The Energy-Time Optimization

Match tasks to energy levels:

- **High-energy periods**: Difficult, important work
- **Medium-energy periods**: Routine tasks, communications, and planning
- **Low-energy periods**: Simple organization and trivial tasks such as adding grocery items to the list, shopping for household items. Even when you're under the weather, these tasks remain manageable.

Trying to do creative work when your brain is fried is like sprinting with ankle weights. Possible, but unnecessarily complicated.

Systems vs. Random Activity

Efficiency goes way beyond time management. It's about *optimizing* and creating *systems and processes* for everything and constantly improving. Successful businesses operate this way. Companies without efficient operations can't scale because chaos doesn't multiply well. This is an art form worth mastering early on.

Apply this personally:

- Morning routine that eliminates decision fatigue
- Meal planning that reduces daily food decisions
- Organizational systems that prevent daily item searches
- Communication templates for everyday situations

Here's what you should remember: you'll discover massive amounts of available time when you sequence activities logically and think systematically. As a former project manager and process-improvement consultant at corporate America's software development space for 18 years, I was trained to create processes for routine tasks and continually optimize them. Don't just do things randomly—engineer every process for maximum effectiveness.

The payoff is real. More time for what matters. Less stress from constant rushing. And honestly? A serious side effect is that once you start thinking this way, inefficiency becomes physically painful to watch.

Your Efficiency Upgrade

This week, identify your three biggest time-wasters:

1. What activities can be batched together?
2. What waiting periods could become productive time?
3. What high-energy tasks are you doing during low-energy periods?

Make one systematic improvement. Watch how this small change creates a ripple effect of better time management throughout your day.

Because when you optimize time, you don't just get more hours—you get more life.

Principle 11: **The Optimization Practice**

Master efficiency through strategic task sequencing and process improvement. Create systems for everything and continuously refine them to maximize results while minimizing wasted effort.

◎ Teach & Thrive

Here are five ways to develop efficiency skills in your children:

1. **Process Mapping Made Fun:** Create visual flowcharts of everyday routines, such as morning prep, homework completion, and bedroom cleaning, showing each step in sequence. Have your kids identify bottlenecks or wasted steps, then redesign the process together for greater efficiency. This teaches them to look at how they do things and find ways to make them better, which is the foundation of ALL productivity.

2. **Strategic Time Blocking:** Teach children to plan activity sequences using visual time blocks to enhance their time management skills. Create daily schedules divided into time periods, then challenge them to arrange activities optimally—considering energy levels, task dependencies, and logical groupings. For younger children, use physical blocks representing different activities to organize in an efficient order.

3. **Multi-Task Training:** Create engaging games that develop simultaneous task management. "Kitchen Efficiency Olympics," where they complete cooking tasks while setting the table and starting other preparations. Time activities separately and combined to demonstrate

intelligent multi-processing advantages. This builds the ability to identify complementary tasks for efficient combination.

4. **Transition Time Optimization:** Help children identify and eliminate wasted time between activities. Create "Transition Checklists" for moving between major daily activities. Measure baseline transition times, then implement improvements to reduce intervals. This develops awareness of how small inefficiencies accumulate into significant time losses.

5. **Resource Management Simulation:** Create age-appropriate activities to develop optimization thinking. For younger children, consider optimizing their bedtime routine to maximize playtime. For older children, consider organizing a pretend store to maximize customer flow. These activities teach them to use what they have wisely to get the best results—the essence of both productivity and investing.

Goal: Develop children who naturally optimize their time and resources instead of randomly reacting to whatever happens next.

PRINCIPLE 12

Have Good Taste

*"Quality is never an accident;
it is always the result of intelligent effort."*

—*John Ruskin*

Why Discernment Determines Your Life Quality

People with good taste—in food, relationships, experiences, and
opportunities—consistently enjoy higher quality lives than those who can't
tell the difference between excellent and mediocre. They also make better
financial decisions because they can distinguish between genuine value
and clever marketing. This isn't about being snobby or pretentious. It's
about developing the ability to recognize genuine quality, which becomes
a superpower that affects every decision you make.

The ability to spot what's actually good—whether it's people,
opportunities, or investments—represents one of the most valuable skills
you can develop. People who master this can identify functional patterns,
copy successful approaches, and apply lessons that consistently create
positive outcomes.

Recognizing excellence is a superpower many people never develop.

Here's the thing: this skill can be developed and improved, just like any other ability. But first, you need to understand some common mistakes that trip up most people's judgment. Don't make these mistakes:

Don't Mistake Poor Quality for Personal Preference

Here's where most people go wrong: they mistake personal preference for quality assessment.

Preferring apples over oranges? Perfectly fine—that's a legitimate taste preference.

Choosing an obviously rotten apple over a fresh, sweet orange? That's not preference—that's broken quality radar.

Yet people do this equivalent exchange constantly. They choose processed food over fresh ingredients, toxic friends over supportive ones, get-rich-quick schemes over proven wealth strategies—all while claiming it's just "what they prefer."

The Restaurant Mastery Example

Why do some people insist frozen shrimp tastes "just as good" as fresh? Because they've never experienced quality, they can't recognize the difference. Their taste buds have been trained on mediocrity.

Meanwhile, someone with developed taste can immediately distinguish between:

- Fresh vs. frozen precooked seafood
- Real flavoring vs. artificial substitutes
- Quality ingredients vs. cheap alternatives
- Skilled preparation vs. microwave shortcuts

This isn't snobbery—it's educated appreciation. Not to mention that the result of poor food choices can cause health issues from years of consuming processed junk masquerading as convenient.

Don't Mistake Subtlety for Weakness

Something light doesn't automatically mean bland. It can be subtle, complex, and incredibly satisfying. Think about expertly prepared sushi— these offer refined experiences that untrained palates might completely miss.

Just because something is intense or overwhelming doesn't make it good. Over-seasoning expired fish with excessive salt and butter isn't flavor—it's masking rot that untrained palates can't detect. The same principle applies everywhere: flashiness often disguises fundamental deficiencies.

Don't Mistake Credentials for Competence

Just because someone has credentials doesn't guarantee quality results. I learned this lesson the hard way multiple times:

- **The Paver Installation Disaster:** Hired a "10-year landscaping company" whose actual workers were googling installation techniques on my project. The company had years of experience; the guys doing the work were on their first rodeo.

- **The Fertility Clinic Reality Check:** Visited the "premier specialists" who wanted to put me on birth control to help me get pregnant—with a $100,000 price tag. (You'll get the full story in a later chapter.)

Experience and expertise aren't always the same thing. The hungry rising star can outperform the established expert who's gotten complacent. I've found that the rising stars—the hungry, talented people still building their reputation—often provide better value than established names coasting on past success.

The Curiosity Advantage

People with good taste ask questions:

- WHY does this food have 47 ingredients when it should have 5?
- WHO actually benefits from this advice?
- WHAT evidence supports these claims?
- WHERE else have I seen this pattern?

Take milk advertising: "Milk builds strong bones!" Sounds great, but which milk? Raw, organic milk from grass-fed cows might have benefits. But does processed milk from hormone-treated cows provide the same nutrition?

Most people never confront these questions because it's harder than just continuing to accept the status quo.

Pattern Recognition for Wealth

Once you start questioning and analyzing, you'll begin to notice patterns everywhere. Some of the most successful businesses follow surprisingly similar models. Here's a business pattern I noticed that applies to massive wealth creation:

Ultra-Successful Companies:

- Don't manufacture products
- Don't maintain inventory
- Own minimal physical assets
- Perform limited manual labor
- Reach mass audiences

Amazon doesn't make products. Uber doesn't own cars. Airbnb doesn't own properties. They're connection platforms that create value through organization and access. There are many, many more businesses following this same model.

Recognizing this pattern could guide your next business venture or investment decision.

Your Taste Upgrade Challenge

This week, develop your quality recognition in one area:

- **Food**: Compare fresh vs. processed versions of the same item
- **Information**: Question one "expert" opinion you've accepted
- **Relationships**: Evaluate whether someone adds or drains energy
- **Opportunities**: Look for the pattern behind successful ventures in your field

The goal isn't becoming impossibly picky—it's developing the discernment that leads to better choices, stronger relationships, and more effective results.

Principle 12: **The Quality Recognition System**

Develop sophisticated discernment across all areas of life—the ability to recognize genuine quality in experiences, opportunities, and especially people becomes the foundation for consistently better choices and outcomes.

◎ Teach & Thrive

Here are five ways to develop quality discernment in your children:

1. **Quality Comparison Training:** Take them to taste genuinely good food alongside average options, then discuss the specific differences they notice. Visit both well-designed and poorly designed spaces, asking them to articulate what makes one more appealing. When possible, let them experience truly well-made items, excellently prepared food, or beautifully designed spaces. Help them understand what makes these experiences special. This trains them to recognize quality in all areas of life.

2. **Marketing Literacy Development:** Transform advertisement consumption into critical analysis. Watch commercials together playing "Spot the Strategy"—identifying emotional triggers, unsupported claims, and persuasion techniques. Ask questions like "What are they trying to make us feel?" and "What claims are they making, and how could we verify if they're true?" This builds resistance to manipulation while developing critical thinking skills.

3. **Pattern Recognition Training:** Point out patterns in successful people's stories, effective business models, or even in nature. Help them see how recognizing patterns in one area can provide insights for

completely different situations. This builds the strategic thinking that identifies opportunities others miss.

4. **Ten-Level Quality Framework:** Teach children to rate quality on a scale instead of just thinking "good" or "bad." Create quality scales with specific criteria for different categories (food, entertainment, friendships, effort). When considering anything, have them place it on a scale (1 to 10) and provide supporting evidence. This replaces simplistic "good/bad" thinking with sophisticated discernment that recognizes degrees of excellence.

5. **Ask "Why" & Decision Consequence Mapping:** Encourage them to ask "why" and "how do you know?" about information they encounter. Create a family culture where questioning is rewarded, not discouraged. This builds the intellectual curiosity essential for good judgment throughout life. Develop foresight by connecting quality choices to long-term outcomes. When making significant decisions, create visual "Consequence Maps" that show the potential results of choosing based on immediate appeal versus fundamental quality. This builds understanding that quality decisions compound into quality lives.

Goal: Train discernment early—children who learn to recognize genuine quality naturally make better choices in relationships, opportunities, and life decisions as adults.

PRINCIPLE 13

What's Good for You IS Good

*"Our lives are fashioned
by our choices.
First, we make our choices.
Then our choices make us."*

—Anne Frank

Learn to desire what genuinely serves your best interests. This isn't about forcing yourself to like kale smoothies when you secretly crave donuts. It's about reprogramming your preferences to align with your goals.

Many people have backwards preference programming—they crave what hurts them and resist what helps them.

The Clothing Store Revelation

When my sister and I owned a women's clothing boutique, we frequently witnessed this mismatch between preferences and reality.

Scene 1: The customer tries on a dress that makes her look absolutely stunning—it beautifully accentuates her figure, transforming her dramatically. Her response? "I don't like the pattern." She chooses something that dulls her appearance because it matches her existing style preferences. The only pattern you should care about is how it makes you look.

Scene 2: Another customer finds THE perfect dress—again, total transformation. She loves it, buys it, and feels incredible. Next day? Returns it because her husband "doesn't like it."

Unless your husband is Oscar de la Renta, his fashion opinion might not be your best guide. (And honestly, have you SEEN my husband's fashion choices? The man wore a Christmas flannel in the spring and dressed our son in a Santa shirt for the Easter egg hunt event. Bless my heart.)

My Simple Clothing Philosophy

I don't care about colors, patterns, or style trends. I care about ONE thing: Does this "do anything for me?" Does it make me look BAM! Amazing? If yes, I will wear it. If not, I don't want it, regardless of how much I might theoretically like it.

Your preferences should serve your objectives, not sabotage them.

The Food Programming Problem

Why do some people consistently choose processed snacks over fresh fruit? Often, it's not a matter of preference—it's conditioning. They've trained their taste buds to prefer artificial flavors, excess sugar, and chemical additives, making real food seem "boring" by comparison.

But here's the thing: taste buds can be retrained. Most people never attempt the retraining process. Your tolerance for salt or bad food works the same as tolerance for alcohol—the more you consume, the more your tolerance increases. The same applies to people who wear perfume. The longer they've worn it, the more desensitized they become, until they're pouring on so much it suffocates everyone else in the room.

The Relationship Reality Check

This principle absolutely applies to the people one chooses to associate with.

In preschool, Max followed two kids around who consistently pushed him away and excluded him from activities. He'd come home disappointed but kept pursuing their friendship.

"You don't need to play with people who don't want to play with you," I explained. "And you don't need to like people who don't like you. Other children would appreciate your friendship."

Teaching your children to prefer people who treat them well isn't cynical—it's self-preservation wisdom.

The Activity Alignment Assessment

Apply this lens to your regular activities:

- **Exercise:** Find movement you actually enjoy instead of forcing yourself through miserable workouts
- **Learning:** Choose skill development that excites you rather than feeling like punishment
- **Socializing:** Spend time with people who energize rather than drain you
- **Entertainment:** Select media that inspires rather than depresses you

When your preferences align with your well-being, achieving your goals becomes a natural process rather than a forced one.

Your Preference Realignment Project

Identify one area where your current preferences work against your best interests:

Food example: If you crave junk food, gradually introduce higher-quality alternatives. Don't go from chips to carrot sticks overnight—try baked sweet potato chips, then roasted vegetables, then fresh options. Train your taste buds progressively.

People example: Notice who energizes you versus who drains you after interactions. Gradually spend more time with energy-givers and less with energy-vampires.

Activity example: If you hate your current exercise routine, experiment with different movement options until you find something enjoyable. Dance, hiking, martial arts, and swimming—there's something for everyone.

The goal isn't forcing yourself to like everything that's "good for you." It's finding good-for-you options that you can genuinely enjoy. But when in doubt, stick to what's good FOR you. It's that simple.

Principle 13: **The Beneficial Preference Shift**

Train yourself to desire what genuinely serves you. Align your preferences with objective benefit rather than programmed responses or fleeting appeal.

◎ Teach & Thrive

Here are five ways to help children develop beneficial preferences:

1. **Taste Expansion:** Train children to recognize quality food by teaching them ingredients, real food versus packaged food, fresh versus old, and taste profiles (sweet, sour, bitter, salty, umami). Compare fresh sweet strawberries to old mushy ones, fresh pizza to day-old pizza. Ask: "Why does this one taste better? What's different?" With repeated exposure to quality ingredients, their palate naturally upgrades. Yes, it's harder work than training kids to eat whatever's given—most parents want easier eaters. But we're not raising garbage disposals who accept any quality. We're raising people who recognize and demand excellence.

2. **Consequence Connection Activities:** Help children connect their choices with results through immediate feedback. Create simple cause-and-effect demonstrations—eating different foods and then tracking energy levels, spending time with friends and then reflecting on mood, and engaging in various activities and then measuring productivity. These direct experiences build understanding that preferences should align with positive outcomes.

3. **Choice Reframing Practice:** Teach children to analyze their preferences using the question, "Is this good FOR me or just good TO me?" Create visual decision frameworks that evaluate options on

both immediate appeal and long-term benefits. This fosters a habit of considering both dimensions, rather than prioritizing immediate gratification.

4. **Value Alignment Checkpoints:** Establish regular reflection periods for children to evaluate whether their preferences align with their stated values and goals. Create a personal "Values Compass" to identify their core values, and then periodically check whether their preferences align with these priorities. This helps them make sure their actions match their values.

5. **Preference Training:** Gradually shift preferences toward better options using small changes. Begin with options 10% better but still appealing, gradually increasing the benefit percentage as preferences adapt. For example, start with minimally processed treats before introducing completely natural options. This "preference training" builds capacity for healthier choices without triggering resistance.

Goal: Raise children whose natural preferences align with their best interests—making good choices feel easy rather than forced.

Be Picky with People Like You're Picky with Food

"You are the average of the five people you spend the most time with."

—*Jim Rohn*

Jim Rohn clearly understood something that most people discover too late: your social environment shapes your destiny more than your education, your talent, or even your family background. Choose your companions like your life depends on it—because it literally does.

Here's what's wild: if you wouldn't eat food that's expired, moldy, or toxic, why would you spend your precious time with people who exhibit those same qualities? That's like being a nutrition expert at the grocery store but a complete amateur in the relationship aisle.

The Programming Power of Your Circle (The Vietnamese Programming Again)

Remember my story about Vietnamese parents obsessing over their children becoming doctors? My brother heard "doctor" constantly and thought,

"Message received." He structured every academic choice around medical school from middle school forward.

The lesson isn't about becoming doctors—it's about social programming. **Repeated exposure to conversation topics and values literally shapes brain development.** If you're constantly around people discussing investments and growth, that becomes your normal. If you're around people complaining about money and making excuses, that becomes your normal, too.

Choose your normal wisely.

Surround yourself exclusively with people who demonstrate positive habits and embody qualities you aspire to develop. As Epictetus advised: "The key is to keep company only with people who uplift you, whose presence calls forth your best."

As we established in Principle 1, exposure to successful people creates awareness of possibilities and plants seeds of ambition. But this goes deeper than inspiration—the people around you literally rewire your brain through constant exposure to their habits, language, and thinking patterns.

The Airport Guy—MillionAIR Effect

I met a 29-year-old with a $100 million net worth, David T. of Texas, who casually mentioned that his private airplane was scheduled for delivery, and he was in the process of purchasing an airport. AN AIRPORT. Like, the whole thing. Not a gate, not a hangar—the entire airport.

His college friend Alex R. shared how David's ambition inspired him to start investing in real estate during their university years. They're both multi-millionaires now, having achieved this at ages when most people are still figuring out how to use their 401(k)s without accidentally buying cryptocurrency.

David also mentioned that when he was young, he declared with complete confidence, "I want to be a billionaire." I have no doubt he'll achieve that goal before most people figure out how to max out their Roth IRA contributions.

Consider the ripple effect of this friendship: Alex could have spent those college years with party friends whose biggest financial ambition was splitting pizza costs evenly and whose idea of an investment strategy was buying lottery tickets. Their late-night conversations would have centered on video games, sports statistics, and debates over whether Die Hard is a Christmas movie.

Instead, he befriended someone with billion-dollar ambitions, and those conversations probably covered market analysis, real estate opportunities, and business development strategies. That association transformed his entire financial future.

Your college roommate's biggest dream becomes your baseline expectation. Choose wisely.

Choose Better Idols

Idolize the people whom you can learn from and become a better version of yourself. People who motivate you. People who can be mentors to you.

My two success idols were the legendary Oracle of investing and the undisputed king of real estate. I've always been fascinated by their businesses, investments, and real estate empire since I was 15.

Don't idolize celebrities and memorize their personal affairs; instead, idolize successful figures you aspire to become, read about their achievements, and draw inspiration from them.

You may say, "Oh, but movie stars and singers are successful." Well, if you want to become an actor or a singer, then by all means, learn how to be a great singer or actor. But most people don't idolize celebrities in this sense.

They idolize and keep up with the gossip—celebrities' dating records—and root for them like they root for their kids at soccer games.

Focus your admiration on those whose accomplishments offer meaningful guidance rather than on entertainment personalities whose lives provide only gossip fodder.

The Partnership Standards Revolution

The lifelong partner you choose can alter your path more significantly than any other single decision. Therefore, it is imperative to carefully select with whom to get involved from the start. It's crucial to know your criteria and have clear expectations.

It may sound like someone killed my romantic cells with anti-romance antibiotics, but believe me, I'm hopelessly romantic and can appreciate all grand romantic gestures. However, you must keep your reality in check and recognize that romance is nothing more than a temporary feeling that can be easily fabricated. This ties back to the principle of having high standards and valuing yourself (previously discussed), so you won't be easily swayed.

You don't have to pick a loser to be romantic or noble. With genuine interest and true appreciation for each other, plus romantic settings, lovely ambiance, fine dinners, and flowers, romance can be reborn over and over again.

Don't explore relationships with someone who is fundamentally misaligned with your standards—this inevitably leads to either a harrowing extraction or compromised standards. Extraction is even more difficult when you're a good person because you want to save them, and it becomes infinitely more complicated when unplanned children are involved.

The best way is to avoid relationships based solely on emotion without strategic assessment.

While specific criteria vary individually, consider these bare minimum standards:

Minimum Standards (Non-Negotiable):

- Treats you exceptionally well and commits to mutual growth
- Values and goals fundamentally align with yours
- Sufficient physical attraction (shallow but honest—chemistry matters. They don't have to look like Thor, but you can't feel repulsed by them in any way, shape, or form—because if you do, then the relationship won't last.)
- No addictions or detrimental habits
- Uncompromising integrity and high character
- Positive mindset
- Stands up for you and has your back no matter what or whom (this includes in-laws)

Warning Signs (Run Immediately):

- Expects unconditional acceptance of negative behaviors without improvement efforts
- Wants you to "love them just as they are" while refusing to grow
- Creates drama, chaos, or constant conflict
- Has different fundamental values about money, family, or future goals

If potential partners don't meet your core criteria, move on immediately.

Don't date from pity or guilt about rejection. Never enter relationships with the primary goal of fixing someone else or hoping they will change.

Don't date for love alone. Don't date someone to save them. Don't date someone if you have to shrink yourself to fit. Reject any situation requiring you to diminish yourself to accommodate the relationship.

If they don't meet your minimum criteria, run. Don't even entertain the idea or let them get close, or you risk getting trapped.

Only date winners who can take you to the next level—losers will consume you and drag you down. Select only partners capable of elevating you while you elevate them.

All this may sound harsh, but you'll see why in Kim's story.

A Tale of Two Paths: A Life of Suffering

Let me tell you a story that I witnessed unfold over two and a half decades—a real-life case study in how one relationship decision can determine the entire trajectory of your life.

To protect their identities, I will change the relationship connection and their names. My father's cousin, whose parents had passed away, moved to a small town in the middle of nowhere in North Dakota. There, she met a man, a knight in shining armor, who came to rescue her with small, trivial tasks that required physical strength. He drove her around (driving wasn't one of her skills at the time), bought her modest gifts, and was charming in that small-town way that feels safe and familiar. He was available, he was interested, and he was RIGHT THERE.

Well, it's hard not to fall for a nice, charming man. She was very young at the time, only twenty-five years old, and if you haven't been around and lived life, twenty-five is quite young. There was much to learn, so much life to experience, and other options to explore before settling for the first available option.

My aunt booked her a flight to visit, hoping it would distract her and encourage her to stay permanently. Remember my parents' wealthy friends and their networks of affluent acquaintances, including those with children who became lawyers and doctors? Vietnamese parents also excel at matchmaking. Well, their friends had a lawyer son whom they arranged for my father's cousin, Kim, to meet. Both families were aligned, and the lawyer, Tanner, was interested in moving forward with an engagement and courtship.

Kim went back to the middle of nowhere in North Dakota, and before she could pack up, the man, Tom, professed his love and convinced her that he would die or kill himself if she left. Red flag alert—run for your life!

Kim was a genuinely kind person, so she was being "nice" (spoiler alert: she's about to learn the principle of "don't be nice"). She stayed.

After she got pregnant, she was physically and mentally abused. She ran to my aunt, trying to escape so she could have her child. Well, he followed, apologized, and shed crocodile tears. Since she didn't want her child to grow up without a father, they moved into a one-bedroom apartment near my parents.

Slowly but surely, he started to reveal that he was a drinker and a compulsive gambler. He had no family, no friends, no savings, no house, no car, and a minimum-wage job that he barely secured. Every penny he made went straight to the casino.

Baby number two arrived, and now the trap was even deeper. She managed to run her own business and became the primary breadwinner while raising her two children. Occasionally, when money was given to Tom to buy something for the house, he would disappear all day and come home empty-handed the next morning.

Twenty-one years later, the kids grew up and moved out. The abuse had stopped years ago, but not the gambling. Tom had nowhere to go, and Kim didn't have the heart to leave or kick him out because he would have nowhere to go. So she's still planning her escape.

BIG mistake. Huge!

What would the path of marrying a lawyer with well-off parents and being in a network of wealth have been like? We'll never know.

Kim's story stuck with me—in my 20s, I made sure to steer clear of any "Tom" types.

Pick WISELY!

The Friend Selection Reality Check

It's better to enjoy your own company doing things you genuinely love than to compromise your authenticity for social acceptance from the wrong crowd.

Find activities you actually enjoy, then connect with others who share those interests. Instead of changing yourself to fit in with random people, maintain your true interests and attract compatible companions.

Your Social Circle Audit:

Energy Assessment:

After spending time with this person, do you feel:

- Energized and inspired (keep)
- Neutral/unchanged (limit)
- Drained and discouraged (eliminate)

Growth Impact:

Does this person:

- Challenge you to improve (essential)
- Support your current level (occasional)
- Encourage mediocrity or bad decisions (dangerous)

Value Alignment:

Do they:

- Share your core values (necessary)
- Respect but differ on some values (acceptable)
- Actively oppose your values (incompatible)

The Strategic Association Action Plan:

Increase time with people who elevate, inspire, and challenge you

Decrease or eliminate time with people who consistently drain, discourage, or oppose your growth.

This isn't about being judgmental—it's about being intentional. I'm not saying to get rid of everyone who doesn't share the same hobbies or interests, or who isn't at your level. I'm referring to the individuals who are toxic to your personal growth and development. You become those with whom you surround yourself. Choose wisely.

Principle 14: **The Strategic Association Principle**

Strategically curate your social environment—friends, partners, and mentors—knowing these relationships fundamentally determine your direction, speed, and ultimate destination.

◎ Teach & Thrive

Here are powerful methods to develop relationship discernment in your children:

1. **Friend Quality Framework:** Teach children to evaluate friendships through systematic assessment rather than random social connections. Create a "Good Friend Qualities List" where they identify what makes someone a quality friend: treats them well, shares similar interests, encourages good choices, includes them appropriately, and resolves conflicts fairly. This teaches them to choose friends intentionally instead of just accepting whoever shows interest.

2. **Energy Impact Awareness:** Help children recognize how different people affect their mood, motivation, and behavior. Track how they feel before and after spending time with various friends. This builds the crucial life skill of recognizing the impact of relationships on personal well-being and achievement potential.

3. **Role Model Selection Training:** Guide children toward admiration of people whose paths offer applicable lessons rather than entertainment figures. Create a "Success Hero Project" where they study someone they genuinely admire, learning specific strategies, principles, or character traits that person applied to achieve their goals. This

teaches them to admire people for their achievements rather than just celebrity status.

4. **Values Alignment Assessment:** Help children understand the critical importance of shared fundamental values. Create regular family conversations about the principles that matter most to your family—such as integrity, kindness, hard work, discipline, education, and financial responsibility—then help children identify which friends and future relationship prospects share these core values. Help them recognize when differences are small preferences versus major incompatibilities that will cause problems. This builds the essential discernment for long-term relationship success and happiness.

5. **Relationship Boundary Development:** Strengthen children's ability to maintain their authentic selves while building social connections, rather than changing their personality or compromising their standards for acceptance. Create "Stay True" challenges that help them practice maintaining their interests, values, and goals when facing social pressure. Role-play situations where friends encourage choices that conflict with family principles or personal goals. This builds the self-respect and confidence necessary to attract compatible relationships rather than settling for whoever accepts them, or becoming a people-pleaser.

Goal: Raise children who thoughtfully curate their social environment, understanding that relationships either accelerate or limit their potential.

PRINCIPLE 15

Don't Be Nice

"People confuse kindness with being nice.
And they're very different.
You can be nice and be passive.
But kindness requires action."

—Daniel Lubetzky

Don't confuse being nice with being good. "Nice" people avoid conflict at any cost—even at the expense of their own well-being and principles (or worse, acting "nice" but not a good person). Good people maintain high ethical standards while appropriately protecting their boundaries.

Never harm others without justification, but never allow others to hurt you in any way.

The "Nice" Person's Dilemma

I've watched my parents be so excessively accommodating that it actually hurts them. Dad struggles to gracefully exit social gatherings when he's ready to leave. Mom once had to rescue him from a contractor who pressured him into signing an inflated estimate simply because Dad felt uncomfortable saying no.

Being "nice" in these situations isn't kind—it's self-destructive and actually enables bad behavior in others.

The Manhattan Food Poisoning Incident

During a business dinner in Manhattan, a colleague pressured me to try an unfamiliar seafood dish despite my obvious hesitation. It wasn't because it was unfamiliar, but more because of the way it was prepared. With highly sensitive taste and smell, I could tell something was wrong, but I felt socially obligated to comply.

"Just try it!" he insisted, practically feeding it to me.

Every fiber of my being rejected that bite, but I forced myself to swallow it and smile rather than appear rude. Six hours later: severe food poisoning that knocked me out for days.

I promised myself: **never again will I try to be "nice"** and consume anything my body clearly rejects, regardless of social settings.

This reflects a broader principle: protecting yourself isn't rudeness—it's appropriate self-protection. Health concerns represent just one domain in which excessive accommodation can cause harm. Safety, relationship, and financial well-being require similar boundary maintenance. When something feels wrong, honor that instinct instead of overriding it to be "nice."

Being Nicely Taken Advantage Of

Timmy goes out with five guys. Everyone orders expensive steaks and multiple drinks, while Timmy gets a modest $30 entrée. When the check arrives, everyone suggests splitting evenly.

Timmy doesn't want to appear cheap, so he agrees—despite this being completely unfair. He pays for everyone else's excess consumption because he's too "nice" to speak up.

This isn't generosity—it's enabling others to take advantage of his conflict avoidance.

The Art of Principled Strength

When someone speaks negatively to you, respond confidently and establish clear boundaries. If they showed no concern about hurting your feelings, you don't need to prioritize protecting theirs when setting necessary limits.

Be polite, but never be a pushover. "Dumb nice" behavior invites exploitation because it signals that you won't protect your own interests.

You don't have to match inappropriate behavior, but you absolutely should address it. You can be a GOOD person without having to be nice. And sometimes being a good person means you can't be "nice".

Remember this: Those with evil intentions seek out those who can be easily taken advantage of. A bully always picks on someone smaller than themselves. "A wolf in sheep's clothing looks for the weakest of the flock." You get the point, right? Or do I need to keep going?

The Taekwondo Code of Honor

Being genuinely good—maintaining high ethical standards while protecting appropriate boundaries—creates better outcomes than being indiscriminately "nice" through conflict avoidance. I appreciate the principles my son's taekwondo class instills—a code that balances respect for others with self-respect, the Master calls it "10 Mental Education":

1. Be loyal to your country.

2. Be loving and show fidelity to your parents.

3. Be loving between husband and wife.

4. Be cooperative between brothers and sisters.

5. Be faithful to your friends.

6. Be respectful to your elders.

7. Establish trust between teachers and students.

8. Think before hurting any living thing.

9. Never retreat in battle.

10. Always finish what you start.

Notice the balance: deep respect for relationships AND unwavering commitment to standing your ground when necessary. It teaches how to be a GOOD person, not a nice person. These ten life-commandments align with my teaching, and they resonate with my core values. Perhaps I might have to frame and hang it in our bathrooms.

The Boundary Training Program

I teach my children: "Never allow anyone to hurt you or bully you in any way. Never hit or bully others, but if someone hits you, you have to handle it and defend yourself (hit them back)—otherwise they'll hit you again tomorrow."

"Move away from people who bother you. Don't stand there and cry. Stop problems before they escalate."

Example: When Evelyn reaches for Max's food, I don't tell him to "be nice" and share. I tell him, "You saw her reaching for your plate. Why did you wait until she took it, THEN cry? Next time, move your plate before she reaches it."

A few days later, I was preparing dinner when I heard Max call out, "Mama!" I walked over to their eating station. Max reported to me, "Evelyn tried to reach for my plate, but I moved the plate away before she got to it. It worked, Mama!" Real-life lessons can happen right at home. A lesson for Evelyn would be a different topic.

Teaching strategic self-protection, not reactive victimhood.

Your Boundary Upgrade Challenge

This week, practice principled strength in one area:

- Say no to a request that doesn't align with your priorities
- Address someone who consistently treats you poorly
- Stand up for your preferences instead of defaulting to others' choices
- Set a clear boundary about your time, energy, or resources

Remember: Being good means maintaining high standards for both how you treat others AND how you allow others to treat you.

The goal isn't to become confrontational—it's to remain unshakeable in your values while being kind to those who deserve kindness.

Principle 15: **The Good Over Nice Approach**

Develop a balanced virtue that combines ethical behavior with appropriate boundary maintenance. Focus on being reasonable and fair rather than being indiscriminately nice at your own expense.

◉ Teach & Thrive

Here are five ways to develop principled strength in your children:

1. **Boundary Recognition Training:** Develop children's ability to distinguish between appropriate and inappropriate requests through scenario-based learning. Create scenarios with age-appropriate situations where children determine whether each request respects or violates reasonable boundaries. This helps them tell the difference between being helpful and being taken advantage of.

2. **Assertive Communication Development:** Teach children to express boundaries respectfully but firmly through graduated practice scenarios. Create a "Response Ladder" with progressively assertive phrases appropriate for different boundary violations—from gentle reminders to clear refusals. Practice through role-play, focusing on calm confidence rather than aggression or submission.

3. **Ability to Recognize Fairness:** Help children develop a clear understanding of reciprocity and fairness in relationships. Show them that healthy relationships have give-and-take with relatively equal respect, effort, and consideration. Discuss examples where this balance is maintained versus those where it is violated.

4. **Self-Respect Reinforcement Rituals:** Create daily affirmation practices that build their self-worth. Have them recite personalized "Worth Statements" during morning routines: "I'm important," "My feelings matter," "I can say no when needed." These should be stated while maintaining eye contact in mirrors.

5. **Balanced Virtue Development:** Help children understand the distinction between kindness and weakness through concrete examples. Use stories and real-life examples, emphasizing that genuine goodness requires both external consideration and self-protection.

Goal: Raise genuinely *good* children—kind to others while maintaining firm personal boundaries and unwavering self-respect.

PRINCIPLE 16

Get What You Want

*"Successful diplomacy
is an alignment
of objectives and means."*

—*Dennis Ross*

One of life's *most* valuable skills is diplomatic influence—the ability
to achieve your objectives without creating resistance, resentment, or
conflict.

What does it mean? When dealing with a situation, being diplomatic
means handling it adroitly, with tact and skill. When saying something
nasty, being diplomatic means delivering your message and having people
say, "Okay."

> It's far better to accomplish your goal than to be
> "right" while walking away empty-handed.

The Truck Trading Lesson

When Max wanted his truck back from his sister, Evelyn, we didn't let him
snatch it away. Instead, we taught him to find another toy and convince
her to trade.

This early lesson in influence versus force set the foundation for a lifetime of getting what you want through cooperation rather than confrontation.

The Activity Center Diplomacy

My husband Johnny took Max to a children's activity center, only to be told they'd reached their 10-child capacity. Johnny didn't argue about policies or fairness. Instead, he created empathy:

"Do you have children of your own?" he asked the staff member.

When she nodded, he continued gently: "Would you mind explaining to a disappointed 4-year-old why he can't join the other children playing?"

His approach invited cooperation rather than defensiveness. Guess who found space for one more child?

The Paver Company Payment Drama

Our HOA sent a fine for gate damage with security camera evidence clearly showing our contractor's truck backing into it. When I called the company owner, Mike, I expected a straightforward resolution since we'd built a good relationship during the project.

"That wasn't our truck," Mike insisted. "That was the third-party delivery service. You'll need to contact them directly."

I felt my logic brain engaging: "But Mike, we hired YOUR company, not the delivery service. You're responsible for the job, everyone you hire, and any damages."

"Sorry, but it wasn't our truck," he repeated, voice hardening.

Then I remembered our conversations about his family, his business, his reputation...

"Mike," I said, shifting approach, "I know you're a good man who values his reputation. Every neighbor on my street has the same yard, and most will eventually want pavers too."

Pause.

"I have a question for you. Would you rather have me recommend your company to all my neighbors, family, and friends? Or would you prefer I share this experience? This isn't about a few hundred dollars anymore—it's about potentially tens of thousands in future business."

Another pause. "You're right. Send me the invoice."

I didn't need to win an argument—I just needed the gate fixed.

My Mother's Pandan Plant Masterclass

My mother purchased a pandan plant for $18, but when she got home, she realized it wasn't pandan—it smelled like ordinary grass. She returned to the nursery with the plant.

"I'd like to return this. It's not actually pandan," she explained.

The sales rep immediately became defensive: "There must be something wrong with your nose if you can't smell it. This is definitely pandan."

"I cook with pandan regularly in desserts and sticky rice," my mother responded calmly. "I know exactly how it should smell and taste."

"This is a business," the rep countered irritably. "Why would we cheat on something like this?"

"I never mentioned cheating," she observed. "I simply said this isn't pandan."

When he claimed they couldn't process refunds because the owner wasn't present, my mother smiled. "Oh, you're not the owner. No wonder." "The owner wouldn't handle this situation this way. Businesses invest a significant amount in advertising and marketing. This is inexpensive advertising for you. Why would you let a situation like this damage your reputation?"

When he offered another excuse about having no cash for refunds because they just opened and she was the first customer, my mother spotted a flowering plant nearby: "Then I'll exchange this plant for that pot of flowers of the same value—$18."

"That pot is $23," he quickly corrected. "The tag says $18, but the sign says $23. We forgot to change the tag."

Mom picked up the flowers and began walking away: "You can either refund me or I'll exchange it for these flowers."

She left with the more expensive plant, smiling—not because she'd "won" an argument, but because she'd achieved her objective without creating an enemy. She "Dale Carnegie'd" it, and she didn't even know it.

The Diplomatic Influence Formula

1. **Understand their perspective** and motivations
2. **Connect to their self-interest** rather than your needs
3. **Create win-win scenarios** whenever possible
4. **Focus on outcomes**, not being right
5. **Maintain relationship health** for future interactions

Dale Carnegie's *How to Win Friends and Influence People* should be required reading for anyone who wants to accomplish anything involving other humans (which is pretty much everything). In fact, it should be mandatory reading for high schoolers, replacing *Romeo & Juliet*.

Your Diplomatic Upgrade Challenge

This week, practice influence instead of force in one situation:

- A disagreement with your spouse about household responsibilities
- A workplace conflict over project priorities
- A service issue with a business
- A parenting challenge requiring cooperation rather than control

Remember: the goal is to achieve your objective, not to prove your point.

Principle 16: **The Diplomatic Influence Principle**

Focus on achieving your objective rather than winning arguments. Master the art of diplomatic influence to accomplish your goals without creating resistance or resentment.

◉ Teach & Thrive

Here are five ways to develop diplomatic influence skills in your children:

1. **Interest-Based Negotiation Training:** Teach children to identify underlying interests rather than focusing on positions. When siblings fight over a toy (positions), help them identify their actual interests (having fun, feeling respected), then find solutions that satisfy both parties' core needs. Teach them that if someone wants something from them and they don't want to give it, don't timidly refuse; ask the other person what they are offering in return. Vice versa, when they want something from someone, they find something that the person wants and trade it. Max and Evelyn practice this every day.

2. **Perspective-Taking Development:** Help children understand others' viewpoints through structured exercises. Create "Perspective Glasses" where children physically put on different glasses representing the perspective of another person in various situations. "What do you think the other person feels?" "How would you feel if that were you?" This builds the empathy they need to influence others effectively.

3. **Influence Approach Selection:** Teach children to choose the right persuasion approach for different people and situations. Create "Influence Toolkits" that utilize different strategies, including logical appeal (facts and reasoning), emotional appeal (feelings and values),

credibility appeal (expertise and trust), and relationship appeal (connection and goodwill). Practice identifying which approach works best in different scenarios.

4. **Win-Win Solution Creation:** Create engaging activities where children can only "win" by ensuring others also benefit. Design trading games where points are earned only when both parties improve their positions. Or create family challenges that require addressing everyone's needs. This teaches them that lasting success comes from mutual benefit, not exploitation.

5. **Diplomatic Language Library:** Help children develop a vocabulary of phrases to achieve objectives without creating resistance. Create flashcards with challenging scenarios on one side and diplomatic responses on the other, such as "That won't work for me, but here's something that might work for both of us" instead of "No, that's a terrible idea." Practice these responses through role-play until they become natural.

Goal: Raise children who can accomplish their objectives through cooperation and influence rather than force and confrontation—a skill that will serve them in every relationship and situation.

Count 1-2-3

> *"Between stimulus and response,*
> *there is a space. In that space is our power*
> *to choose our response. In our response*
> *lies our growth and our freedom."*

—*Viktor Frankl*

Before responding to any situation, action, or message, count to three.
Handle every circumstance with grace and composure, regardless of
provocation.

The Waffle Wars Wisdom

Max and Evelyn were fighting over waffle pieces. I gave each a plate
and was distributing pieces between them when Evelyn wanted one I'd
intended for Max. To prevent conflict, I gave it to her. Max immediately
snatched it back, triggering an escalating argument over who deserved
which piece first.

After everything had settled, Max took a bite and declared, "Mom, I don't
like it."

**Lesson learned: Don't fight so hard for something you might not even
want.**

How many adults do this same thing? Argue passionately for positions, relationships, or opportunities they haven't even properly evaluated. Emotional reactivity rarely serves your actual interests.

The Pointing Finger Incident

Max was saying something when Evelyn disagreed and pointed at him while clearing her throat. Max didn't like the pointing and told her to stop. Evelyn, being three and committed to her stance, continued pointing while closing her eyes with dramatic flair.

This escalated Max to full meltdown mode over... a pointing finger.

Real talk: How often do we adults do the same thing? Get completely hijacked by minor provocations that have zero actual impact on our lives?

The Pause Advantage

Professional environments particularly reward emotional control. The ability to:

- Receive criticism without defensiveness
- Navigate conflicts without escalation
- Maintain composure under pressure
- Think before speaking when triggered

These skills directly impact financial outcomes through better negotiation results, stronger professional relationships, and wiser decision-making under stress.

The Three-Count System

When someone asks you a question, pause briefly before responding. This prevents reflexive answers and allows thoughtful responses.

When you hear something disagreeable, pause and ask for clarification before reacting. Often, initial interpretations are wrong anyway.

When something doesn't actually harm you, recognize there's no need to react emotionally at all.

The Emotional Hijack Prevention

Emotional mastery doesn't mean suppressing feelings—it means preventing emotions from hijacking your executive function. You can:

- Acknowledge your feelings
- Feel them fully
- Choose optimal responses despite those feelings

The goal is to maintain your ability to choose responses rather than being controlled by instinctive reactions.

My Kids' Emotional Training

When Max gets upset over something minor, I ask: "Did that actually hurt you or just bother you?" If it just bothered him, we would discuss whether it's worth getting upset about.

When Evelyn has a meltdown, we practice: "Take three deep breaths. Tell me what happened. What do you need? The more you yell, the more difficult it is for people to understand you."

Building their pause muscle early so they can handle bigger challenges later.

The Grace Under Pressure Advantage

- People who maintain composure during conflicts:
- Make better decisions
- Preserve relationships
- Project confidence and competence
- Often get better outcomes because others want to work with them

People who react emotionally to every trigger:

- Make poor decisions in heated moments
- Damage relationships through unnecessary conflicts
- Appear unstable or immature
- Often get worse outcomes because others avoid dealing with them

Your Emotional Sovereignty Challenge

This week, practice the three-count system:

1. **Before responding** to any question or request
2. **Before reacting** to criticism or disagreement
3. **Before engaging** in unnecessary conflicts

Notice how this simple pause changes both your responses and others' reactions to you.

The three-count technique works beautifully for daily irritations—such as spilled drinks, rude comments, and minor frustrations. Master this skill on the small stuff because it builds your emotional muscle for life's bigger challenges. Allowing minor frustrations to constantly cloud your emotions will have a long-term impact on your everyday well-being.

What happens when you skip this training entirely and let primary emotions actually take control of your decisions and actions? The consequences aren't just uncomfortable feelings—they're real damage that can last for years.

Master the pause on small stuff to build strength for significant challenges.

Principle 17: **The Emotional Sovereignty Principle**

Master your emotional responses through deliberate pause and conscious choice. Those who control their emotions rather than being controlled by them make better decisions, maintain stronger relationships, and achieve superior results.

◉ Teach & Thrive

Here are five ways to develop emotional mastery in your children:

1. **Emotional Vocabulary Expansion:** Develop children's ability to precisely identify emotions beyond basic labels. Practice identifying specific emotions in stories, situations, and personal experiences. Research shows that accurately naming emotions reduces their intensity and makes them easier to manage, building emotional awareness.

2. **Pause-Process-Respond Protocol:** Teach children specific sequences for handling emotional triggers. Create visual "Response Steps" showing: 1) Pause (take three deep breaths), 2) Process (identify emotion and cause), 3) Choose (select constructive response).

3. **Physiological Regulation Techniques:** Help children use their bodies to calm strong emotions. Create age-appropriate "Calm-Down Steps" with physical strategies like deep breathing, tensing and relaxing muscles, or focusing on what they can see, hear, and touch.

4. **Emotion-Outcome Connection:** Help children see how their emotional responses affect outcomes through real examples. Show them how different emotional responses lead to different outcomes

in specific situations. After emotional episodes, help them identify the connections between their emotional reactions and the resulting consequences.

5. **Perspective Expansion Practice:** Help children view situations from multiple perspectives, which naturally reduces emotional reactions. Practice identifying at least three different interpretations for any emotionally triggering situation. This fosters cognitive flexibility, which naturally moderates emotional intensity.

Goal: Raise children who can feel their emotions fully while maintaining the ability to choose their responses—the foundation of both personal success and strong relationships.

You'll Lose If You Let Your Emotion Win

> *"You have power over your mind—*
> *not outside events. Realize this,*
> *and you will find strength."*
>
> —Marcus Aurelius

Marcus Aurelius clearly never had to deal with family drama that escalates into years of lasting damage. But the man understood something crucial: when you lose the battle for emotional control, you don't just feel bad— you make bad decisions that create real consequences.

When you control your emotions, you win. When emotions control you, you lose.

We just learned in Principle 17 how to pause for daily irritations—the waffle wars and pointing fingers. Now let's talk about what happens when emotions actually win and drive your actions. This isn't about feeling frustrated for a few minutes; this is about letting emotions control your decisions and watching the damage compound for months or years.

Here's what separates successful people from everyone else: they don't sweat the small stuff. But more importantly, they don't sweat the big stuff either. They've mastered the art of emotional sovereignty—making stressful situations disappear through mental discipline rather than letting stress multiply through emotional reactivity.

The Millionaire's Stress Test

Wealthy people don't sweat the small stuff, and they make big issues small. You can't be successful if you can't make stressful things disappear.

Take Trump, for example—someone everyone knows—love him or hate him (this isn't about politics), the man has more issues to deal with than any regular person. Legal battles, constant media scrutiny, business pressures, political opposition, impeachment trials, asset seizing attempts, and family drama played out on the world stage. This isn't meant to scare you or tell you not to pursue success or have big dreams. It's the opposite—if you have big dreams and want to achieve them, you *must* learn how to not sweat the small or big issues.

Think about it: if you sweat the broken AC or traffic jam, then it would be tough to deal with issues that are 10x the magnitude.

But here's the key—successful people don't develop a bigger stress tolerance; they grow better at stress *processing*. They've learned to separate facts from emotions, problems from catastrophes, and temporary setbacks from permanent defeats.

The moment you let emotions drive your decisions, you've already lost the game.

When Emotions Win, Everyone Loses
(The Sister Chronicles)

Let me tell you about a time I learned this lesson the hard way, and how letting my emotions get the best of me turned a trivial situation into a relationship disaster.

My cousin, my sister, and her new boyfriend evacuated from a hurricane and came for a weekend trip. It was exciting—a chance for the family to meet him, and it had been a while since my ride-or-die, dynamic-duo-partner sister came back to town.

We all ended up going out together that evening. I had to leave early to pick up Max, who was three at the time. Since everyone else was having fun, I told them they could stay—no reason for everyone to end their Saturday night early just because I had mom duties.

What I didn't realize: my sister had different expectations about how the evening should end. She hadn't communicated her preference, and I hadn't thought to ask.

What started as a simple miscommunication became an ego battle. She felt I'd undermined her wishes. I felt attacked for trying to be considerate. Instead of pausing to understand each other, we both let our emotions take over. We found reasons to be offended, made up justifications for our feelings, and let something completely trivial spiral into lasting damage.

Looking back, if we had just paused and discussed it gracefully, there were many ways to fix or defuse the issue—even after the fact. But we didn't. And the damage compounded.

I realized that how significant something feels is directly related to how much weight you put on it. The more weight you assign, the more it affects your emotions. And as humans, we make up reasons to justify our feelings, which only compounds the problem.

Most of the time, it's not *what* happened—it's *how* you let the emotion take control and *how* you handle it. This "conflict" wasn't even really a conflict. It was a minor coordination issue that we turned into relationship damage through poor emotional management and failure to sympathize.

The Rental Turnover Disaster

Here's another example of letting emotions prevail over logic.

I had a rental property with tenants moving out. I was overwhelmed by everything happening at once, plus the disappointment that the place didn't get listed as requested. Therefore it didn't get under a lease contract before the current tenants moved out to avoid the vacancy gap. I let my emotions take over and made a crucial mistake: I decided to "not deal with it" for a few days to defuse the stress.

By not dealing with it for a few days—meaning I didn't think about it—I forgot to turn the utilities back on under my name after the tenants moved out. When my realtor started showing the property, there was no electricity and no water.

No water is inconvenient, but no electricity in the Texas heat? You can imagine the consequences. Not exactly the ideal showing conditions for attracting quality tenants.

This wasn't about the house, the listing issue, or the tenants. This was about how letting emotions cloud judgment creates a cascading series of adverse effects. When I let stress overwhelm me rather than process it systematically, I created additional problems that took more time, energy, and money to fix.

The lesson isn't about property management—it's about emotional management. When you don't control your emotions, they control your actions, which control your outcomes.

The True Cost of Emotional Reactivity

When your emotions win, the damage extends far beyond the immediate situation. Emotional reactivity creates:

- **Relationship Damage:** Arguments escalate beyond their original scope, trust erodes, and temporary disagreements become permanent rifts.

- **Financial Consequences:** Poor decisions made in emotional states often have expensive consequences that could have been avoided with clear thinking.

- **Personal Stress:** The most important damage is to your own peace and well-being. You can't think clearly, make good decisions, or be happy when you're constantly battling problems that weren't even significant issues in the first place.

- **Lost Opportunities:** While you're dealing with drama created by emotional reactivity, you're missing chances to develop, build, and advance.

The irony? Most situations that trigger strong emotional responses could be easily minimized or made to disappear entirely with just a moment of strategic thinking.

The Emotional Control Framework

Here's what I wish I had done with both the sister conflict and the rental property situation:

- **Step 1: Pause and Assess.** Before reacting, ask: "Is this actually a problem, or is this just something I don't prefer?"

- **Step 2: Focus on Outcomes.** "What do I actually want to happen here?" Focus on solutions, not grievances.

- **Step 3: Choose Your Battles.** "Is this worth my energy and time?" Save your emotional investment for things that truly matter.

- **Step 4: Respond Strategically.** Handle the situation in a way that gets you closer to your desired outcome, not just immediate emotional satisfaction.

In the sister situation, my desired outcome was family harmony and including everyone in a fun evening. Escalating the issue served neither of my goals. Getting offended about my sister's feelings really spiraled out of control.

In the rental situation, my desired outcome was to quickly get quality tenants. When water is already under the bridge, there is no need to stay frustrated.

Teaching Children Emotional Control

The earlier you learn this skill, the more successful and peaceful your life becomes. I'm teaching Max and Evelyn that there's a difference between feeling emotions (which is natural and healthy) and letting emotions make your decisions (which is costly and unnecessary). When they get upset about something, we practice the pause: "Take a breath. Is this actually hurting you, or is it just annoying? What do you want to happen instead? What's the smartest way to get that result?"

This isn't about creating emotionally cold children—it's about making children who can acknowledge and manage their feelings without being overwhelmed by them.

Principle 18: **The Emotional Control Framework**

Recognize and prevent emotions from completely hijacking your decision-making process. When emotions drive actions, they create cascading damage across relationships, finances, and personal well-being that compounds over time.

◉ Teach & Thrive

Here are powerful methods to develop emotional control in your children:

1. **Situation Scale Assessment:** Help children tell the difference between real problems and simple preferences. Create a "Big Deal Scale" ranging from 1 to 10, where individuals rate situations before reacting emotionally. Practice with daily scenarios, such as spilled juice (2) and a friend's rude comment (4), versus truly significant issues like family safety (9-10). This teaches them to respond appropriately—not overreacting to small things while taking big issues seriously

2. **Outcome Focus Training:** Redirect children from problem-focused to solution-focused thinking through strategic questioning. When they encounter frustrating situations, consistently ask: "What do you actually want to happen here?" and "What's the fastest way to get that result?" This cultivates the sophisticated thinking pattern that distinguishes effective people from reactive ones.

3. **Emotional Pause Protocol:** Build in a deliberate pause before responding through practice. Establish a family rule where everyone counts to three before responding to anything that triggers strong emotions. Practice this during neutral situations so it becomes automatic during stressful ones. Create visual reminders without

embarrassing children. This teaches them to choose their response instead of reacting emotionally.

4. **Battle Selection Framework:** Teach children to evaluate whether situations deserve their emotional energy. Help them understand that emotional energy is limited and valuable—spending it on trivial issues leaves them depleted for essential matters. After emotional episodes, review what that energy could have been used for instead. This teaches them to spend their emotional energy wisely.

5. **Hero Response Modeling:** Build better response habits by learning from people they admire. When children face challenging situations, ask: "What would [someone they admire] do in this situation?" Help them identify calm, effective people from their lives, stories, or media who handle stress well. This gives them better examples to follow instead of just reacting, building emotional maturity.

Goal: Prevent emotional takeovers that create lasting damage (major emotional control for high-stakes situations)

PRINCIPLE 19

Cheapest Lessons

"Smart people learn from their mistakes.
But the real sharp ones learn from
the mistakes of others."

—*Brandon Mull*

Learning from others' mistakes is the most cost-effective, the cheapest—
these lessons come completely free, without the painful tuition of personal
stress.

Study not just what successful people do, but what unsuccessful people do.
Often, knowing what NOT to do also provides valuable guidance.

The Working-From-Home Scam Prevention Course

A friend shared her experience with a how-to-make-serious-money
course scam. The operation appeared completely legitimate—featuring
a professional video, convincing documentation, and polished sales
representatives.

She lost $10,000 before realizing the whole thing was fake.

The lack of details about the course was a subtle warning sign she dismissed, as were the pressure tactics she ignored. Her experience provided me with a comprehensive fraud-prevention framework without personally losing a penny.

That free education was worth far more than $10,000.

The Technology Stock Disaster

Another acquaintance trusted a friend and didn't extensively research a new technology company before investing a significant portion of her savings. Just before an unexpected regulatory announcement, the stock plummeted 60%.

While she eventually recovered financially, the emotional toll and opportunity cost were substantial. Her transparent sharing of the experience—including her decision-making process, the signals she missed, and her subsequent diversification approach—provided me with practical investment wisdom that I would have otherwise gained only through a similar loss.

The Business Partnership Breakdown

A colleague started a business with his best friend without clear agreements about responsibilities, decision-making, or profit sharing. When the company became successful, their friendship imploded over issues of money and control.

Watching their partnership destroy both their business and their relationship taught me more about proper business structure than any MBA course could. Now I know precisely what legal and communication frameworks to establish BEFORE entering any business relationship.

My Parent Credit Card Machine

My parents, who speak only basic English and are generally "nice" (but remember not to operate solely from "niceness"), were tricked into signing a contract with a third-party company that provides credit card machine services for small businesses. The salesman somehow convinced them, and they felt compelled to sign without reading all the fine print, relying solely on his promises. Later, they discovered they had to pay exorbitant fees—not just transaction fees—but also a rental fee for an unreasonably long period.

When my sister and I launched our brick-and-mortar business, we applied their hard-learned lesson.

Rule of Thumb: when someone tells you to sign something right here, right now, that's a sign to sleep on it.

The Efficiency of Vicarious Learning

Instead of linear advancement through personal trial and error, you can incorporate centuries of collective human experience into your decision-making.

This principle applies across every domain:

- **Financial** decisions (learn from others' investment mistakes)
- **Relationship** choices (observe what destroys vs. strengthens partnerships)
- **Career** moves (study both successful and failed career transitions)
- **Health** decisions (learn from others' lifestyle consequences)
- **Parenting** approaches (see what creates confident vs. anxious children)

The Story Mining Process

When others share experiences, listen for:

- **The thinking process** that preceded outcomes (often more valuable than outcomes themselves)
- **Warning signs** they missed or ignored
- **Decision frameworks** they used (or wish they had used)
- **Environmental factors** that influenced the results
- **Alternative approaches** they considered or now recommend

My Investment in Other People's Stories

I actively cultivate relationships with people willing to share both triumphs and failures transparently. These conversations provide priceless insights that help me navigate similar situations without experiencing the same costly consequences. And what better "bedtime" stories than real stories with lessons learned?

Learning from others, not only what to do but also what not to do, can help prevent costly mistakes.

When your family and friends ask you, "How are you?" don't just answer with "fine". When people always answer "fine", I stop asking them because I already know their answer.

When appropriate, please share your wins and any hiccups you are facing. When you share your wins, it gives you momentum and opens doors for opportunities. And chances are that when you share your challenge, others can offer solutions. For example, when I was dealing with the breastfeeding issue, instead of saying "I'm doing okay" and moving on to the weather, I straight-up told my friend that my nipples were clogging and cracking. She recommended solutions and encouraged me not to stop breastfeeding. She literally said, "You can do it in Summer!" So I sought out a lactation consultant, got the issue fixed, and breastfed my second baby for a year; otherwise, I would have quit at month 2 like I did with my first baby.

Sharing wins and losses benefits you and others.

Some of my most valuable "free education" came from:

- Parents sharing honest parenting successes and failures
- Entrepreneurs explaining business decisions they regret
- Investors describing their worst (and best) financial moves
- Couples discussing what strengthened or weakened their relationships

The Mentorship Connection

This principle naturally complements formal mentorship (Principle 28). Beyond structured mentor relationships, create a practice of thoughtfully analyzing successes and failures you observe in others.

Your Vicarious Learning Assignment

This week, actively seek one "expensive lesson" you can learn for free:

- Ask someone about their biggest professional or financial mistake
- Research a failed business in your industry and analyze what went wrong
- Study a successful person's path and identify patterns you can replicate
- Listen to friends' relationship experiences and extract applicable wisdom

"Learn from the mistakes of others.
You can't live long enough to make them
all yourself."

—*Eleanor Roosevelt*

Remember: Other people's expensive mistakes can become your free education—if you're wise enough to learn from them.

Principle 19: **The Vicarious Learning Advantage**

Systematically harvest wisdom from others' successes and failures. Create a practice of extracting valuable lessons from every observed experience, thereby gaining benefits without paying personal costs.

◉ Teach & Thrive

Here are five ways to develop vicarious learning skills in your children:

1. **Story Mining Protocol:** Turn entertainment into education by finding the lessons. Create a "What Did You Learn?" discussion session for books, movies, and real-life accounts, using prompts such as: "What mistake did the character make?" "What was the lesson learned?" and "How could they have achieved better outcomes?" You can learn from movies consistently—well-crafted films with meaningful narratives, not degrading entertainment.

2. **Decision Consequence Library:** Help children collect examples of others' experiences. For older children, create physical or digital "Decision Journals" where children document significant choices and outcomes they witness in friends, family members, characters, or public figures.

3. **Failure Analysis Discussions:** Destigmatize mistakes by regularly analyzing high-profile failures in age-appropriate contexts. Select news stories, historical events, or business case studies where things went wrong. Use consistent "Failure Analysis" questions where children identify what happened, why it happened, and how it could have been prevented. This teaches them to spot patterns in mistakes.

4. **Mentorship Interview Practice:** Teach children to learn from experienced people through thoughtful conversations. Create "Expert Question Templates" with questions that bring out valuable insights: "What's your biggest regret in this area?" "What decision gave you the best return?" "What do you know now that you wish you'd known earlier?" Help them practice these conversations with relatives before approaching other wisdom sources.

5. **Consequence Visualization Exercises:** Help children imagine possible outcomes before making decisions. When facing choices, guide them through "Future Vision" exercises where they imagine the results of different options based on patterns they've observed in others. Create simple templates with three columns: "Choice," "Likely Outcome," and "How I Know" (requiring them to cite specific examples). This teaches them to think ahead without having to learn the hard way. We often ask our kids, "What do you think will happen?" and tell them, "If this happens, then would you be okay with it?"

Goal: Develop children who systematically harvest wisdom from every observed experience, gaining benefits without paying personal costs—the ultimate learning efficiency.

Celebration Penalty

"The moment you think you've won is the moment you start losing."

—*Kobe Bryant*

Celebrating achievements reinforces success pathways and fuels motivation for continued progress. However, excessive celebration often carries hidden penalties that can undermine your success.

In college football, scoring teams that display excessive celebration receive penalty flags. Life operates by the same principle: when celebration exceeds appropriate boundaries, negative consequences quickly follow.

The Alcohol Equation

Consider alcohol consumption: one drink beyond your personal limit triggers cascading penalties—physical illness, impaired judgment, recovery downtime, potential safety risks, and possible relationship damage.

These consequences far outweigh any momentary enjoyment from the excess.

The Social Event Strategy

Apply this principle to gatherings and professional events: arrive promptly but depart before exhaustion or diminishing returns set in. Never be the person who "closes down the bar" or lingers after an event has effectively concluded. Later in the book, we'll talk about the concept of "not everything applies 100%". Obviously, this doesn't apply if you are at a family or friend's event and stay back to help with the cleanup.

There's a sweet spot in every celebration—recognize it and honor it.

Premature Celebration Downfalls

Premature celebration is considered excessive—celebrating before an achievement is complete isn't just undeserved, it's about letting your guard down, and there could be expensive losses. As you have seen, it has played out in sports.

- **LSU Tigers vs. Tennessee Volunteers 2010:** The Volunteers lost to the LSU Tigers in one of college football's most memorable and chaotic finishes. Tennessee's players and fans started celebrating, thinking they had won, believing the clock had expired. But officials reviewed the play, only to overturn the call and give LSU one final, untimed down. LSU running back Stevan Ridley then scored the game-winning touchdown.

- **Falcons' Premature Celebration:** The Atlanta Falcons celebrated prematurely and lost Super Bowl LI to the New England Patriots. Falcons players were reportedly "dancing and hooraying" in the locker room during halftime, but the Patriots staged an improbable comeback, forcing overtime and winning the game.

The Resource Allocation Reality

This principle extends beyond celebration to encompass resource management in general. In every domain, identify the optimal investment point before returns diminish:

- **Workout duration**: Effective exercise vs. overtraining injury risk
- **Work hours**: Productive effort vs. burnout and error accumulation
- **Social time**: Enjoyable connection vs. social exhaustion and economic cost
- **Leisure time**: Earned relaxation vs. becoming a couch potato

> It's okay to overdo and overperform, but don't overplay, overstay, overdrink, overspend, or you will end up being overly broke.

My Kids' Party Wisdom

When we attend children's birthday parties, I watch for the moment when my kids' excitement peaks—usually after the cake but before they experience overstimulation meltdowns. That's our exit cue.

We leave while they're still happy rather than staying until they're exhausted, overwhelmed, and emotional. They associate the event with positive feelings instead of ending on a negative note.

The Diminishing Returns Warning Signs

Learn to recognize when additional investment begins producing declining returns:

- **Energy drops** despite continued activity
- **Quality decreases** in work or attention
- **Enjoyment fades** and obligation takes over

- **Negative consequences** begin accumulating
- **Recovery time** starts to outweigh the benefit time

Strategic Celebration Guidelines

- **Celebrate proportionally:** Match the celebration intensity to the significance of the achievement. Completing regular homework deserves acknowledgement, not a parade.
- **Celebrate meaningfully:** Focus on memorable experiences rather than excessive consumption or extended duration.
- **Celebrate consciously:** Notice when celebration shifts from enjoyment to obligation or begins creating adverse side effects.
- **Celebrate strategically:** Use celebration to reinforce positive behaviors and build motivation for future achievements, not to escape or avoid reality.

The Peak Moment Exit Strategy

Master the art of leaving experiences at their peak rather than enduring their decline. This applies to:

- Social gatherings (leave while still enjoying yourself)
- Vacation activities (end on a high note)
- Entertainment (stop before you get bored or overwhelmed)
- Alcohol consumption (a little may help you loosen up, and a little more gives you a buzz, but going over your limit can have enormous consequences—risk of injury, or even fatal consequences)
- Food consumption (apply the Japanese concept of *hara hachi bun me*, mindfully eating about 80% to prevent overeating)

Strategic celebration means acknowledging achievements in ways that reinforce success patterns without creating counterproductive consequences. Celebrate meaningfully but appropriately, then redirect energy toward your next objective rather than extending the celebration beyond its optimal duration.

This concept requires balanced implementation. Insufficient celebration fails to create the necessary motivation and reward circuits, while excessive celebration depletes resources that are better directed toward future achievement. The discipline to maintain this balance distinguishes consistently successful individuals from those who experience intermittent success followed by setbacks.

Your Celebration Optimization Challenge

This week, practice strategic celebration:

1. **Identify** one area where you typically over-celebrate or overindulge
2. **Recognize** the optimal stopping point before negative consequences
3. **Practice** ending activities while still enjoying them
4. **Notice** how this affects your overall satisfaction and energy

Remember: The goal is a sustainable celebration that enhances rather than detracts from your continued success.

Principle 20: **The Celebration Equilibrium**

Acknowledge achievements with appropriate celebration while avoiding excess that creates penalties. Recognize when additional celebration begins producing diminishing or negative returns and redirect energy toward future goals.

◉ Teach & Thrive

Here are five ways to develop strategic celebration skills in your children:

1. **Milestone-Reward Celebration:** Teach children to align their celebration scale with the significance of achievement through real examples. Create visual "Celebration Scales" showing appropriate reward levels for different accomplishments. Minor achievements (completing regular homework) get small acknowledgments; significant milestones (mastering difficult skills) warrant more substantial celebration. This builds understanding that rewards should be proportional to the accomplishment.

2. **Quality Over Quantity Framework:** Help children distinguish between meaningful celebration and excessive indulgence. For example, too many sweets can lead to obesity. Playing too long at the water park when it's scorching hot can cause them to become dehydrated and sick. This teaches them the difference between meaningful celebration and overdoing it.

3. **Recovery Rate Awareness:** Help children see how celebration choices affect subsequent performance. After various celebratory activities (staying up late, consuming sugar, and extended TV time), have them

track their energy levels, focus, and mood the following day using simple rating scales.

4. **Optimal Exit Training:** Teach children to recognize optimal endpoints in enjoyable activities before diminishing returns set in. Create "Peak Moment Exit" concepts—recognizing when experiences reach their best point and leaving while they're still great. Practice this at amusement parks, parties, and other enjoyable events. This builds good judgment in leaving experiences at their peak rather than letting them decline.

5. **Celebration-Achievement Connection:** Help children document both accomplishments and subsequent celebrations, including how rewards are related explicitly to achievements. This makes celebrations more meaningful and connected to real achievements instead of creating a sense of entitlement. This can be done through journaling or pictures for younger kids.

Goal: Develop children who celebrate achievements in ways that enhance rather than undermine their continued motivation and success.

PRINCIPLE 21

Showing Off Is for Losers

"A lion doesn't have to tell you it's a lion."

—*African Proverb*

Never perform self-destructive acts to gain social approval. Whether chugging entire bottles of liquor, making dangerous physical choices, or purchasing status items beyond your means, these approval-seeking behaviors undermine rather than enhance your position.

Showing off is the recipe for losing—lose your health, lose your life, lose your money.

The Social Pressure Financial Trap

Social pressure frequently manifests in expensive ways:

- Feeling obligated to pay for group dinners because of pressure
- Purchasing name-brand items rather than equivalent alternatives that better align with your financial situation
- Upgrading your lifestyle to match people whose incomes far exceed yours

- Taking expensive vacations or buying luxury items to maintain appearances

These moments represent critical decision points: Will you maintain financial discipline or compromise for temporary approval?

A Costly Group Dinner for the Show-Off Guy

Remember Timmy's expensive dinner situation? He got cornered into paying for other people's tabs because he was "nice".

This time it's at the expense of being a show-off. Chad went to dinner with his girlfriend and two other couples. It was their anniversary, and the other couples decided to split the cost as an anniversary gift, saying that Chad had let them crash his dinner. Chad insisted on picking up the tab for the whole table.

Here is the reason why showing off is for losers: these couples are multi-millionaires, while Chad is struggling to meet obligations. But he wanted to pay because he felt ashamed, or wanted to prove that he "has it". The issue here is not that he picked up the tab for the table. Being able to pick up tabs easily is a luxury not everyone can afford. **Generosity is a privilege that not everyone can give.**

It wasn't generosity—he didn't have the capacity to be generous—it was financial self-sabotage to mask insecurity and project an inflated sense of worth.

What's even worse than this? Feeling obligated to pay to avoid appearing "cheap", to show off and convince others you're a "big shot", or to appear wealthier than you are. This mindset would send the pursuit of financial freedom to its grave. Detrimental! Don't show off by pretending to look rich—that's how you lose.

The Authentic vs. Show-Off Distinction

Consider a child proudly showing friends a new toy versus an adult conspicuously displaying luxury items to impress others. The child's behavior reflects natural excitement, while the adult's often masks insecurity.

There's a difference between sharing joy and seeking validation. Two people can be showing something, but one is a show-off and one isn't. The line is very fine, and it depends on the inner intention:

The authentic person shows a new toy with the same inner-child intention as a five-year-old showing it to his friends, full of joy and excitement, genuinely ecstatic to share.

The show-off person doesn't say, "Look at my watch! Look what I got!" but instead buys and wears them as proof and validation, in the hope of impressing others.

This realization became clear to me when my sister pointed it out. Once, my sister and I had a conversation about how much progress her ex-boyfriend had made. We were saying we're so glad Nick is doing well. Then she made a comment suggesting that he buys nice things and wears his watch to show off because he didn't have much before. I instinctively questioned my habit, saying, "Well, I buy and wear nice things." She clarified, "No, you buy because you LOVE nice things and you APPRECIATE nice things. You don't care what other people think. When you share, you are sharing the appreciation." "He buys because he wants to impress others," she added.

I love sharing good things and great deals. And that's the difference.

The "Nice Things" Reality Check

Here's the truth about impressive possessions: confident, successful people rarely feel the need to prove anything through material displays, even though they drive a Rolls. Successful people do wear nice things, but because they appreciate them as opposed to seeking approval or trying to prove something that they are not.

Meanwhile, people struggling financially often prioritize image over substance—driving luxury cars they can't really afford while living in apartments without basic furnishings, or carrying designer bags while pinching everywhere else.

Don't be that person with a Louis Vuitton purse and a Ramen noodle budget.

Never attempt to impress others at personal expense. Pretending to have more money than you actually do and trying to keep up with the Joneses is how to go broke. Avoid diminishing your standards or authentic self to gain acceptance from groups that don't align with your values. The highest-value relationships develop from mutual respect for authenticity rather than conformity to external expectations.

This principle extends beyond specific choices to your overall approach to possessions and achievements. Display genuine enthusiasm for your interests and acquisitions without seeking validation. The distinction between sharing and showing off lies in intention—one comes from genuine joy, the other from a desire for validation.

The Validation Independence

When you're secure in your worth, you don't need external validation through:

- **Material possessions** that drain your financial resources

- **Risk-taking behaviors** that could harm your health or safety
- **People-pleasing decisions** that compromise your values or wellbeing
- **Status competitions** that distract from genuine goal achievement

Instead:

- Pick up a new skill
- Figure out how to make more money for real
- Perform a random act of kindness

Your Anti-Show-Off Challenge

This week, practice authentic confidence:

1. **Say no** to a social expense that doesn't align with your financial priorities
2. **Choose quality** over brand name in one purchase decision
3. **Share genuine enthusiasm** about something you love without seeking impressive reactions
4. **Set a boundary** about your time or resources, rather than automatically accommodating others

Remember: People who need to prove their worth usually don't have much worth to prove. People who actually have worth rarely feel the need to prove it.

Principle 21: **The Authentic Validation Principle**

Maintain unwavering commitment to your authentic values rather than seeking external validation through compromise. Make choices based on internal standards rather than external pressures, cultivating relationships that appreciate your genuine self.

◎ Teach & Thrive

Here are five ways to develop authentic confidence in your children:

1. **Approval Dependency Assessment:** Help children identify when they're making choices based on others' approval rather than internal values. Help them create awareness by asking: "What I Really Want" and "What I Think Others Want." Max got a new pair of sandals, and he told me he can't wait to go back to school to show Alice his new shoes and have her say, "Wow." It may be just inner-child excitement, but you know my alert kicked in. I told Max, "I know you love your new shoes, and it's okay to show them to your friend, but it doesn't matter if she likes them or not, as long as you do. And you don't need to care if other people like it or not because it's not theirs."

2. **Peer Pressure Resistance Training:** Build children's ability to maintain boundaries despite peer pressure through progressive practice. Create role-playing scenarios where children practice declining inappropriate requests or suggestions. Provide specific response templates: "That doesn't work for me," "I'm not comfortable with that," or "I have to pass."

3. **Status Symbol Analysis:** Strengthen children's critical thinking about buying things to impress others. When encountering obvious

status-driven purchases or behaviors (in media or real life), guide analysis with questions: "Why do you think they bought/did that?" "What were they hoping others would think?" "Was this choice aligned with their authentic values?" This teaches them to tell the difference between what they truly want and what they buy to impress people.

4. **Value Alignment Checks:** Teach children to evaluate choices against core values before making decisions. Create personalized "Values Compasses". When making decisions, have them check alignment: "Does this choice reflect who I really am?" "Would I make this same choice if no one else knew about it?" This builds confidence from within instead of seeking approval from others.

5. **Authentic Expression Practice:** Build children's confidence in being themselves through practice. Create "True Self" opportunities where children share actual interests, preferences, and ideas in increasingly challenging contexts. Begin in completely supportive environments (such as family) before gradually expanding to less familiar settings (friends, then public). This teaches them to stay true to themselves in any situation.

Goal: Raise children who derive confidence from their character and capabilities rather than external validation or material possessions—creating genuine security that others' opinions can't shake.

PRINCIPLE 22

Treat Your Body Like a Temple

"Take care of your body.
It's the only place you have to live."

—Jim Rohn

Health is your most valuable asset—it makes everything else possible. Without physical well-being, all other accomplishments lose their significance.

> Having abundant time but inadequate resources limits enjoyment. Having substantial resources but insufficient time prevents full utilization. Having both time and money but serious health issues is meaningless.

The Resource Priority Matrix

Consider these scenarios:

- Time + Money + **Poor Health** = Limited enjoyment and capability
- Time + Health + **Limited Money** = Some options

- Money + Health + **Limited Time** = High-quality experiences in compressed timeframes
- **Health + Time + Money** = Unlimited potential for an extraordinary life

Good health provides the capacity to build wealth, which in turn enables you to reclaim time and attain exceptional experiences.

You Only Get One Body

This isn't a lease agreement where you can trade up to a newer model. You get one body for your entire lifetime, and every decision either invests in or divests from its long-term health and well-being.

Protect your body vigilantly:

- Avoid introducing harmful substances
- Implement comprehensive self-care practices
- Listen attentively to your body's signals
- Exercise consistently and appropriately
- Fuel yourself with quality nutrition
- Avoid overeating to maintain optimal health and physique

Avoid or limit consuming packaged foods. You won't experience immediate consequences, but consistent consumption over time—day after day, year after year—gradually damages your body in numerous ways. This is precisely how people age prematurely, looking 60 when they're only 40 (Premature Aging 101).

The 80% Rule Revolution

Enjoy great food as one of life's great pleasures, but consume it in moderation. Eat enough to appreciate the experience and sustain yourself without overeating, which can lead to discomfort or health consequences.

I remind myself to eat like my kids—they naturally eat just enough to sustain them until the next meal, not a bite in excess.

My military uncle promotes a valuable eating philosophy: never eat until completely full. The Japanese concept of *hara hachi bu*—eating until 80% sated—offers profound health benefits through mindful, moderate consumption, which include effective weight management, improved digestion with reduced discomfort, and others.

Implementing this approach from childhood can create lifelong patterns of healthier eating. Consider the cumulative impact of even slight overeating at every meal for decades—the consequences compound dramatically.

The Daily D.O.S.E. Health Investment

Wellness experts refer to the four happiness chemicals as D.O.S.E.:

- **Dopamine** (reward chemical): Released through task completion, self-care activities, achievement recognition, and quality sleep
- **Oxytocin** (bonding hormone): Released through physical touch, meaningful conversation, pet interaction, and acts of kindness
- **Serotonin** (mood stabilizer): Released through sunlight exposure, meditation, time in nature, reflective journaling
- **Endorphins** (natural pain relievers): Released through exercise, massage, laughter, and dark chocolate consumption

Make sure to treat your body like a temple and give it a good daily DOSE of happiness.

Establish practices generating these beneficial neurochemicals naturally:

- **Morning sunlight** exposure for serotonin
- **Physical movement** for endorphins
- **Quality nutrition** for sustained energy
- **Meaningful connections** for oxytocin
- **Achievement recognition** for dopamine

Love your body. Take care of it.

Your Health Foundation Challenge

This week, implement one health-optimizing practice:

- **Nutrition:** Eat until 80% full rather than completely satisfied
- **Movement:** Add 30 minutes of daily physical activity you actually enjoy
- **Recovery:** Establish consistent sleep and wake times
- **Environment:** Spend time in nature or natural sunlight daily
- **Mindfulness:** Practice brief meditation or gratitude reflection

Remember: Without health, nothing else achieves its full potential value. Prioritize physical well-being as your foundational asset—everything else depends on this essential resource.

Principle 22: **The Ultimate Priority Principle**

Establish physical well-being as your top priority, recognizing that all other achievements depend on this fundamental resource. Implement comprehensive self-care practices that protect and enhance this irreplaceable foundation.

◎ Teach & Thrive

Here are five ways to develop health prioritization in your children:

1. **Body Appreciation Guide:** Teach your children about physical being. Create special "Body Gratitude" rituals where children acknowledge specific things their bodies allow them to experience or accomplish. This builds the mindset that health is their most valuable asset rather than a burdensome obligation. Create a "Love Your Body" guideline— what do you need to do if you love your body?

2. **Sensation Awareness Training:** Help children recognize and respond to their bodies' signals through regular check-ins. Create "Body Signal Check-ins" where children pause briefly during meals, activities, or rest periods to notice their physical sensations. Guide them with specific prompts, such as "What's your energy level?" "Where do you feel tension?"

3. **Body Fueling System:** Transform children's relationship with food to body-power-based thinking. Create a "Power Food Chart" showing food choices that help the body function optimally—different foods affect energy, focus, mood, and physical capability.

4. **Recovery Tracker:** Help children understand the crucial role of recovery in overall health. Help track their performance on specific tasks (physical or mental) when well-rested versus when tired. This builds understanding that rest isn't merely the absence of activity but an essential component of high performance.

5. **Health Investment Visualization:** Create "Future Self Timelines" that show how today's health habits impact future possibilities. For younger children, focus on near-term effects (having energy for tomorrow's activities); for older children, extend to longer-term impacts—vividly showing examples (pictures) of a person's appearance and performance. I show the kids this every day when we come across real-life examples. This teaches them that health is their most important long-term investment.

Goal: Develop children who naturally prioritize their physical well-being, understanding that health is the foundation that enables everything else they want to accomplish in life.

PART 2 SUMMARY

Fundamental Habits

Installing the Operating System for Success

Principle 8: Good Habits Pay Off | *The Habit Installation Framework.* Make habit-building itself a habit. Your daily patterns ultimately determine your destination.

Principle 9: Collect Rocks | *The Acquisition Mindset.* Develop the collector's mentality early. The psychology of acquisition and accumulation naturally transfers to wealth building.

Principle 10: Build a Tent | *The Resourcefulness Mindset.* Cultivate resourcefulness and creative problem-solving. Consistently ask "how" questions to develop innovative thinking.

Principle 11: Don't Wait for the Eggs to Boil | *The Optimization Practice.* Master efficiency through strategic sequencing and systematic optimization. Create systems for everything and continuously improve them.

Principle 12: Have Good Taste | *The Quality Recognition System.* Develop sophisticated discernment in all areas of life. The ability to recognize quality prevents costly mistakes and identifies opportunities for improvement.

Principle 13: What's Good for You IS Good | *The Beneficial Preference Shift.* Align your preferences with what genuinely benefits you. Learn to desire what serves your long-term interests.

Principle 14: Be Picky with People Like You're Picky with Food | *The Strategic Association Principle.* Strategically curate your social environment. The people you surround yourself with can redirect your path and reshape your destiny.

Principle 15: Don't Be Nice | *The Good Over Nice Approach.* Be a good person, fair and just, rather than indiscriminately being "nice". Maintain ethical behavior while protecting appropriate boundaries.

Principle 16: Get What You Want | *The Diplomatic Influence Principle.* Master diplomatic influence to achieve objectives without creating resistance. Focus on outcomes rather than being "right."

Principle 17: Count 1-2-3 | *The Emotional Sovereignty Principle.* Control emotional reactions through the pause-and-think system. Master emotional sovereignty to prevent feelings from being completely hijacked by minor provocations.

Principle 18: You'll Lose If You Let Your Emotion Win | *The Emotional Control Framework.* Emotional mastery prevents poor decisions and preserves relationships. Prevent emotions from completely hijacking your decision-making process. Emotional control leads to better outcomes and relationships.

Principle 19: Cheapest Lessons | *The Vicarious Learning Advantage.* Learn from others' successes and failures. Extract valuable lessons from observed experiences without paying personal costs.

Principle 20: Celebration Penalty | *The Celebration Equilibrium.* Celebrate appropriately without excess. Recognize when additional celebration produces diminishing returns.

Principle 21: Showing Off Is For Losers | *The Authentic Validation Principle*. Maintain authentic values rather than seeking external validation through compromise. Make choices based on internal standards.

Principle 22: Treat Your Body Like a Temple | *The Ultimate Priority Principle*. Establish physical well-being as your highest priority. All other achievements depend on this fundamental resource.

Formula for Success & Freedom

PRINCIPLE 23

You Need to Be an Expert

> *"An investment in knowledge pays the best interest."*
>
> —*Benjamin Franklin*

You don't need to be an expert in everything, but you absolutely must develop sufficient knowledge in any domain where you make significant decisions. Even when hiring specialists, your baseline understanding determines whether their services meet appropriate standards.

Because here's the uncomfortable truth: not all experts are actually experts. And some experts are expertly bad at their jobs.

The Paver Installation First Rodeo

Our newly built house came with all grass—no patio area—and I wanted to create an outdoor paradise with beautiful pavers. After researching proper installation techniques—such as base preparation, drainage requirements, edge constraints, and laying patterns—we hired a company with a decade of experience and numerous large-scale projects.

You know, actual "experts."

Plot twist: expertise doesn't always trickle down to the people doing the actual work.

After the crew started laying pavers, I noticed a fundamental procedural error when observing them from my window. Instead of facing their work area and progressing forward with clear visibility, they worked BACKWARD—stepping onto unprepared areas and digging behind them for the sand, creating depressions they then had to repeatedly fill. This backward approach produced uneven surfaces with noticeable high and low spots throughout the installation.

It was like watching someone try to paint a ceiling while standing on the wet paint.

When I explained the issue and requested that they adjust their technique, they looked at me as if I'd suggested they defy gravity. When the problem persisted, I called the owner.

"But we've been in business for 10 years!" he protested.

"Yes, you have been doing it for 10 years, but your workers appear to be in their first rodeo," I replied. "And you guys skipped the step of screeding the sand. So now you guys keep having to dig to refill, then have to refill the area he dug previously."

This principle extends beyond home improvements to every significant aspect of life. Consider my experience with fertility specialists.

The Fertility Joke

After trying for our second child for six months, concerned about my advancing age, I researched potential issues. I consulted my obstetrician, who ran preliminary tests showing normal results before advising me to seek a fertility clinic. I consulted the city's "premier" clinic—supposed to be the best.

The specialist, with his impressive credentials and confident demeanor, delivered devastating news: "You're in the 'unknown' category. At your age, your chances are 2-5% naturally, but we can improve that to 12-20% with IVF."

Then came the grocery store analogy that made me use the entire box of tissues: "Imagine your ovaries like a grocery store your age with nothing new coming in since it opened—only items going out. What do you think the quality of that canned soup is?"

Through my tears, I managed to respond: "What about whiskey, like Louis XIII? That gets better with age."

He laughed, but still pushed for immediate intervention. He highlighted that my chance of success would increase significantly, showing statistics. He advised that the longer I waited, the lower the chance would be due to my age.

Something didn't add up for me (but could add up to $75,000 for them), and they had already prescribed birth control and wanted me to start immediately. But why would I need to be on birth control? Doesn't that seem counterproductive to conception?

My discernment system instinctively rejected the pressure. I remained confident in my health, supported by normal test results, and I questioned the entire IVF process. An unfortunate side effect of years in corporate America working on process creation and improvement—I'd been trained to question the process and dissect every system. An incurable trait.

Here's the hidden truth: they control the timing so scheduling the egg retrieval procedure is more convenient for the clinic. I was hoping to extract the eggs as a precaution while still trying to conceive naturally. This is why you must understand the process, even if you don't perform the procedure yourself. Don't mindlessly follow so-called experts.

After careful consideration of the invasive procedures, expense, and relatively modest statistical improvement, we decided to maximize our natural opportunities through optimal timing, nutrition, and lifestyle adjustments. One month later, BAM! Pregnant! My eggs were like whiskey!

Here's what he didn't account for: statistics don't predict individual outcomes, especially when no issues exist.

The "expert" wasn't necessarily wrong according to population data, but he never bothered to determine whether I was an exception. He simply applied a statistical formula that served his success rates, showing no genuine interest in my specific situation. The incentive structure was transparent: a $75,000 procedure guaranteed favorable outcomes for his practice metrics, while exploring natural conception offered him nothing but time investment with uncertain results. I'd naively assumed a fertility specialist would prioritize the patient's best interest—exhausting natural options before recommending expensive interventions. Instead, I discovered a system where doctors unthinkingly follow protocols that optimize their statistics, treating patients as interchangeable data points rather than individuals.

I can provide examples of expensive "expert" tax strategists and CPA firms where you end up with interns handling your filings, but I think you get the point.

Be an Informed Client

These experiences underscore a crucial principle: you need not become an expert in everything, but you must develop sufficient knowledge in areas where vital decisions are made. This understanding enables you to critically evaluate professional advice, distinguish between statistical generalizations and individual circumstances, and recognize when proposed solutions align with your specific situation. Sometimes you even must be an expert, training others to do the work for you.

The Expert vs. Competence Problem

Just because someone has credentials, experience, or impressive marketing doesn't guarantee quality results:

- **The 20-year roofing company** whose actual workers googled installation techniques on your project
- **The prestigious dental clinic** that assigns your procedure to yesterday's graduate
- **The expensive tax firm** where interns prepare your returns

Often, the hungry rising star outperforms the established expert who has become complacent. As I mentioned in the earlier chapter, I have found that sticking with the *rising stars* is the best approach.

Your Informed Client Strategy

Develop sufficient knowledge to (DARE U ID):

- **Distinguish between statistical generalizations** and individual circumstances
- **Ask intelligent questions** that reveal actual competence levels
- **Recognize when proposed solutions** align with your specific situation
- **Evaluate professional advice** critically rather than accepting it unquestioningly
- **Understand** the process and the purpose of each step.
- **Identify red flags** that indicate inexperience or poor judgment

The Research Investment

Before any significant decision, invest time in understanding the basics. You don't need to become a master contractor, but you should understand proper installation procedures. You don't need medical school, but you should research your condition and treatment options.

This knowledge protects you from:

- Unnecessary procedures or services
- Substandard work quality
- Inflated pricing for standard services
- Solutions that don't address your actual needs

The Rising Star Verdict

True excellence isn't about how long you've been doing something—it's about the pride and passion you bring to every task.

A rising star is someone who has proven talent—not decades in business, but it's not their first rodeo. It's easy to assume that experts hold all the answers, but experience alone doesn't guarantee mastery. Often, the freshest talents—the rising stars—bring hunger, pride, and relentless commitment that create the best results. They bring passion and drive to outperform and build trust. Rising stars also offer better value and a more competitive price because they're still building their reputation rather than capitalizing on it.

Always stick with the RISING STAR!

Why the Rising Star Approach:

- **Experts are prohibitively expensive.** Premium prices often reflect reputation, not proportional value.
- **Experts don't prioritize smaller budgets.** Your project gets delegated to junior staff while you pay expert rates.

- **Many "Experts" often coast on past reputation.** Success breeds complacency—they no longer need to prove themselves.
- **Rising stars are hungry.** Every project matters to their future, so they bring passion and drive to exceed expectations.
- **Rising stars offer better value.** Competitive pricing and full attention because they're earning trust, not capitalizing on it.

Your Expert Evaluation Challenge

This week, become an informed client in one area:

- Research a service you're considering purchasing
- Learn the basic quality standards for the work you're having done
- Understand the key questions to ask potential service providers
- Identify the warning signs of inexperience or incompetence

Remember: Your job is to become expert enough to recognize real expertise and protect yourself from fake expertise.

Principle 23: **The Informed Client Advantage**

Develop sufficient knowledge in any domain where you make significant decisions, even when employing specialists. Your baseline understanding determines your ability to evaluate advice, recognize quality, and select appropriate solutions.

◉ Teach & Thrive

Here are five ways to develop informed decision-making skills in your children:

1. **Research Skill Training:** Help children develop information-gathering abilities. Help children research increasingly complex topics before making decisions. For younger children, this might involve comparing three toy options; for older children, researching family vacation destinations or major purchases can be a valuable activity.

2. **Expert Evaluation Framework:** Teach children to thoughtfully assess advice rather than accepting it automatically. Develop simple "Expert Assessment" templates with questions: "What experience supports their opinion?" "Do they explain why, not just what?" "Do they acknowledge limitations?". This builds respectful skepticism skills.

3. **Domain Knowledge Bank:** Help children identify knowledge areas most relevant to current and future decisions. Show them different life domains (health, education, finances, and relationships) and the baseline understanding required in each. For young children, teach them simple everyday skills, such as patching a hole in their shirt, sewing a button back on, making a cake, and fixing a hole in the wall.

Emphasize the proper procedure and the process. This builds a passion for learning and understanding how things work.

4. **Alternative Perspective Practice:** Help children consider opposing viewpoints by examining different approaches. When encountering expert recommendations or mainstream advice, implement "Different View Challenges". This builds intellectual flexibility and protection against groupthink.

5. **Knowledge Application Simulation:** Help children turn information into practical decisions through realistic scenarios. For example, researching pet care before creating comprehensive care plans addressing specific challenges. This bridges gaps between abstract information and practical application.

Goal: Develop children who can evaluate expertise intelligently, ask the right questions, and make informed decisions rather than unquestioningly trusting authority.

Dominate

> *"Be so good they can't ignore you."*
>
> —*Steve Martin*

You can be good at many things, but you must select one domain where you develop exceptional capability and establish a clear professional identity.

The Identity Advantage

Think about universally recognized specialists: Gordon Ramsay has culinary excellence. Tony Robbins rules personal development. Warren Buffett defines value investing.

Each is known for mastery of one specific domain, and it's their identity. I'm not saying that you need to become that big and famous. I'm saying the return is high when you become an expert in *your* field. It's important to have a domain of expertise. Make it your identity and dominate it.

The Specialization vs. Informed Client Balance

This principle complements rather than contradicts the principle of the informed client (Principle 23). Maintain sufficient understanding across multiple domains to make informed decisions while developing comprehensive mastery in your chosen specialty.

Think of it as being conversationally fluent in several languages while being completely fluent in one.

Dominate Your Domain, Own Your Identity

To truly own your identity, it's not enough to be a jack of all trades; you must dominate one domain so entirely that it becomes your kingdom. This mastery fuels your confidence, sets you apart with premium value, and empowers you to make your most significant impact.

Owning a domain creates an *identity*, which brings certainty, significance, and the ability to contribute at the highest level.

Certainty creates confidence—you know who you are, no matter what life throws at you. Significance gives you a sense of connection to your purpose and values. And having the ability to contribute naturally drives you to step up and make an impact.

The Expertise-Income Connection

Here's why specialization creates wealth: **focused expertise generates greater value than diffused knowledge.**

A general practitioner might be competent across many areas, but the specialist commands premium pricing because they solve specific, valuable problems better than anyone else.

Identity Moment

In my first couple of projects at IBM, I served in a "general" role, and honestly, I felt completely lost. I'd watch the subject-matter experts and the senior executives, and I'd think, "*That's what real expertise looks like.*" Meanwhile, I was just... there.

I started as a project manager assistant, managing budgets and forecasts. The training was valuable, sure, but I didn't feel any sense of ownership. I wasn't contributing anything meaningful. Without a clear identity—not just professionally, but holistically—you drift. You feel like you don't matter. That was me on the first couple of projects: floating around, contributing little, convinced I could be removed from any project at any moment, and nobody would even notice.

Then one day, a manager pulled me aside. "You need to pick a domain," he said. "An area where you want to become a subject matter expert." He'd built his entire career in Quality Assurance and loved it—*loved* it. That conversation changed everything.

I offered to help with testing. I explored software testing, then stepped into the role of business analyst. Eventually, I advanced to QA Manager, overseeing the entire QA process and team—an integral part of the software development cycle. Here's the thing about QA: all builds, releases, and go-lives *must* go through the QA process and obtain that stamp of approval. Nobody releases without us.

Being a subject-matter expert, owning your domain gives you certainty— an unshakable foundation—knowing exactly where you stand and what you bring to the table. It gives you a deep sense of meaning and respect. Your expertise and mastery allow you to solve real problems, creating genuine value for the team, the project, and others.

Specialization Selection Strategy

Choose your domain based on:

- **Market demand**: Skills that generate substantial compensation

- **Personal alignment**: Areas where your interests and aptitudes intersect
- **Growth potential**: Fields with expanding opportunities rather than declining prospects
- **Passion sustainability**: Disciplines you can remain enthusiastic about long-term

The Deep vs. Wide Decision

While others spread their efforts across multiple interests, commit to going DEEP in your chosen area:

- **Real estate specialist**: Become the definitive expert in your specific real estate niche
- **Technology specialist**: Master your particular technology stack completely
- **Creative specialist**: Develop exceptional capability in your specific creative medium

Your Domination Action Plan

1. **Choose your domain** based on market demand and personal alignment
2. **Study the masters** who've achieved exceptional results in this area
3. **Develop systematic expertise** through deliberate practice and continuous learning
4. **Build your reputation** as the go-to person in this specific domain
5. **Command premium compensation** based on your distinctive value creation

Remember: Being exceptional at one thing creates more opportunities and income than being adequate at many things. Master one domain, create your identity.

Principle 24: **The Identity Specialization Strategy**

Select and dominate a specific domain through concentrated focus and continuous development. Establish a clear professional identity based on exceptional capability rather than scattered competence.

◎ Teach & Thrive

Here are five ways to develop specialization skills in your children:

1. **Depth-Before-Breadth Philosophy:** Build skills through deep mastery. Help them understand that reaching higher elevations on one mountain creates more value than climbing the foothills of many mountains. Guide them through selecting one skill area for intentional depth development with specific advancement plans.

2. **Identity Development Framework:** Help children see how developing skills shapes who they become. Create progressions from "Interested In" to "Learning About" to "Becoming" in chosen focus areas. This shows them that becoming an expert shapes their identity and what they can offer the world.

3. **Expert Study System:** Help children understand specialization better. Select age-appropriate experts in fields that align with their interests. Identify common patterns: early interest, systematic practice, mentor relationships, progressive challenge acceptance. This shows them the focused work required to become an expert.

4. **Deliberate Practice Protocol:** Create specific practice sessions focused on deliberate improvement, with clear feedback and steadily

increasing difficulty. This teaches them that becoming an expert requires focused practice, not just repetition.

5. **Value Creation Connection:** Show children how specialization creates real value through clear examples. Compare beginning piano players with accomplished pianists, or casual sports participants with dedicated athletes. This shows them that going deep creates far more value than staying shallow.

Goal: Guide children toward selecting and developing deep expertise in chosen domains, understanding that specialization creates more value and opportunities than scattered competence.

A Left-Hand Job

*"The only thing
that is constant is change."*

—*Heraclitus*

In today's rapidly changing world, job security has become a rare commodity. Virtually anyone can lose their position with minimal notice, regardless of performance, tenure, or company loyalty.

It's essential to develop backup capabilities before you need them.

The "Who Moved My Cheese?" Reality

One of the most impactful business books I've encountered is "Who Moved My Cheese?"—a seemingly simple yet profound work that offers wisdom about navigating modern economic realities.

The core lesson: **recognize when your current situation is changing and proactively seek new opportunities before your existing ones disappear.**

Consider Blockbuster's fate. Their "cheese" (video rental business model) disappeared when streaming technology emerged. Instead of recognizing this shift and adapting, they maintained their traditional approach until obsolescence rendered them irrelevant.

This taught me that single-source dependency—whether on one employer, client, or revenue stream—creates unnecessary vulnerability.

The Single-Point-of-Failure Disaster

I once worked for a company that derived 85% of its revenue from a single client in the oil and gas industry. When that sector experienced a downturn, its primary client halted the project and cut spending.

The result? Massive layoffs. Eventually, 95% of employees lost their positions.

The company shrank to just the founder and a skeleton crew because it lacked diversification, and their cheese got moved. This was living proof that single-source dependency can lead to disaster.

My Husband's Adaptation Strategy

My husband runs a successful digital marketing agency, but I regularly remind him to watch for industry shifts that might move his "cheese." The digital marketing landscape changes rapidly—due to algorithm updates, platform changes, and new technologies.

He stays ahead by:

- Continuously monitoring industry trends
- Diversifying service offerings
- Maintaining multiple client types
- Investing in ongoing education
- Building systems that can adapt quickly

We call him "J. Fast" because he pivots quickly when changes occur. Also, because he's obsessed with supercars.

The Left Hand (Backup) Job Strategy

One of my confidence sources (beyond family support) is knowing I have immediately employable skills that generate income regardless of economic conditions. This safety net allows appropriate risk-taking while protecting against worst-case scenarios.

It seems like we are contradicting each other again, but it's actually about building a fortress that protects your confidence foundation and financial structure. You need to be an informed client, you need to be a specialist—having in-depth expertise in one area, and you need to build a safety net by having a backup job. This will make you unshakable.

Your backup job should be:

- **Schedule flexible** (you control when you work)
- **Location independent** (available anywhere you might live)
- **Consistently demanded** (needed regardless of economic conditions)
- **Quickly accessible** (you can start earning within days or weeks)

The Confidence Multiplier Effect

Having a reliable backup doesn't just provide financial security—it creates psychological freedom. When you know you can generate income quickly if needed, you can:

- **Take calculated risks** in your primary career
- **Negotiate from strength** rather than desperation
- **Leave toxic situations** without financial panic
- **Pursue opportunities** that might not work out

Your Adaptation Preparation Plan

1. **Assess your vulnerability**: How dependent are you on single income sources?

2. **Monitor change indicators**: What trends might affect your industry or role?

3. **Develop backup capabilities**: What skills could generate quick income if needed?

4. **Test your backup**: Can you actually earn money with these skills now?

5. **Stay adaptation-ready**: How quickly could you pivot if necessary?

The Cheese-Moving Survival Kit

Whether you're employed or running a business, always:

- **Diversify your dependencies** (multiple clients, have multiple income streams or skill sets)

- **Monitor environmental changes** (industry trends, economic indicators, technology shifts)

- **Maintain backup options** (alternative opportunities, emergency skills, financial reserves)

- **Practice adaptation** (regularly try new approaches, stay flexible, embrace change)

Remember: In a world where change is the only constant, your ability to adapt quickly and maintain multiple options determines your survival and success.

The question isn't whether your cheese will move—it's whether you'll be ready when it does. Make sure you have "cheese" coming from different sources.

When your financial security doesn't depend on a single source, you operate from a position of strength rather than desperation. You negotiate better terms. You pursue opportunities with confidence. You exit unfavorable situations without panic. Multiple income streams don't just protect you—they position you to capitalize on opportunities others must pass by.

> Make certain you have income flowing from multiple sources. This isn't merely advisable; it's essential for both building wealth and achieving genuine freedom.

Principle 25: **The Strategic Security System**

Create resilience through proactive adaptation, diversification, and backup capabilities. Develop immediately employable skills that provide both practical security and psychological confidence during inevitable transitions.

◉ Teach & Thrive

Here are five ways to develop adaptability and security planning in your children:

1. **Change Readiness Training:** Create "Change Simulation" activities where they practice adapting to unexpected modifications in rules, environments, or plan for the weekend. Start with small changes and gradually increase difficulty as they improve.

2. **Diversification Visualization:** Help children understand risk distribution through concrete demonstrations. Create "Security Portfolio" exercises using physical objects—for younger children, not putting favorite toys in one basket or snacks in one secret hiding spot; for older children, diversifying hypothetical investments or income sources. Use visual aids to show how spreading resources across multiple areas provides protection if one thing fails.

3. **Backup Skill Planning:** Develop children's awareness of backup capabilities through strategic skill development. Help them identify and develop at least two distinct, valuable capabilities. Help them understand that while specialization creates primary value (Principle 24), backup capabilities provide essential security. Emphasize skills with consistent demand regardless of economic conditions or technological changes.

4. **Trend Monitoring Practice:** Help children spot changes that might affect future opportunities. Create age-appropriate "Trend Tracker" activities where they see changes in areas of their interests. For younger children, this might involve noticing shifts in playground games; for older children, observing technological or cultural developments.

5. **Scenario Planning Exercises:** Teach children to create backup plans. Implement regular "What If" scenarios such as for the weekend plan, exploring potential changes and appropriate responses. For example: "What if your favorite activity became unavailable?" or "What if the store is closed when we get there?" Guide them to create specific, clear plans instead of vague ideas.

Goal: Develop children who view change as normal and manageable, rather than threatening, and are equipped with both primary capabilities and backup options for any situation.

Think Long Enough and You Shall Receive

"Thoughts become things.
If you see it in your mind,
you will hold it in your hand."

—Bob Proctor

People generally receive what they deeply desire and persistently pursue. This represents the essence of manifestation—not passive wishing while binge-watching Netflix, but active intention aligned with consistent effort.

If you don't have something that you said you wanted, you probably didn't really want it intensely enough to take the necessary actions.

The Manifestation Reality Check

Many people claim to want financial success, but their choices demonstrate that they prioritize immediate comfort over wealth building. They claim they want to be rich, yet they spend every paycheck on depreciating assets.

Similarly, many express a desire to be fit but consistently choose consumption patterns and activity levels that drive the opposite outcome.

They want abs while eating like abs are made in the kitchen of a donut shop.

> **Real manifestation requires alignment between your stated desires and your actual behaviors.**

The RAS Programming System

The reticular activating system (RAS)—the brain network connecting conscious and subconscious processing—can be trained through visualization to recognize and pursue desired outcomes.

Located at the brain stem and receiving input from multiple sensory pathways, this mechanism serves an alerting function that can be programmed through intentional focus.

The red car effect is a perfect example of how RAS works—once you decide you want a red car, you suddenly notice red cars everywhere.

Think of it as your brain's personal search engine. Whatever you consistently search for starts showing up everywhere.

My Manifestation Magic Story

Around age 15, I became fascinated with "owning lots of land, buildings, and houses" (I didn't even know the term "real estate" yet). I had no clear path forward, but the vision was crystal clear.

When I entered Louisiana State University, I pursued a degree in information systems, entirely unrelated to property ownership. My immediate aspiration was securing a position that allowed for luxurious travel with expenses covered.

My first post-graduation job placed me in a tiny town in the middle of nowhere with one traffic light—the opposite of my cosmopolitan dreams.

I felt trapped in a professional dead-end territory. I started reading some business books and visualizing my dream job of prestige. Without knowing it, I was actually "manifesting".

Here's where manifestation works its magic...

During training, I connected with a colleague, and we kept in touch through the company's internal chat. I expressed to him how I felt trapped in that town. One day, he mentioned his friend at a major technology company. Without having met me, he forwarded my resume to this connection, who shared it with her manager.

After a brief phone interview, I received an acceptance letter requesting relocation to Washington, D.C.

The luxury IBM journey began: a corporate credit card with a $99,999 limit, covering all expenses—flights, hotel, rental cars, meals, everything—including dry cleaning. I could travel anywhere my heart desired on weekends. Nine out of ten times, it was a first-class flight, plus I had private car service on speed dial. My vision of luxurious business travel took an unexpected turn. I will never forget these three names, and I am forever grateful to my former coworker, Mark S., his friend Cheryl M., and her manager, Eric D.

This experience dramatically elevated my standards, accelerated my professional development, and connected me with exceptional colleagues. But more importantly, IBM helped me shape my identity (professionally and holistically) and provided the missing link to my real estate dreams by connecting me with investing colleagues.

The Universe Alignment Effect

Years later, a client whom I worked with on one of the IBM projects introduced me to "The Secret," which described the manifestation process I had unknowingly employed. Subsequently, my husband—boyfriend at the time—took me to Bob Proctor's event, which further validated these principles.

(Yes, I got my picture with Bob Proctor—because meeting success mentors matters more than celebrity selfies!)

While my experience may seem ordinary, imagine what might have resulted from even more ambitious visualization.

The Manifestation Formula

Effective manifestation requires:

- **Crystal Clear Vision:** Specific, detailed mental pictures of desired outcomes. You have to help the universe to help *you*.
- **Emotional Intensity and Intention:** Genuine desire that motivates consistent action
- **Aligned Behavior:** Daily choices that support rather than contradict your vision
- **Persistent Focus:** Maintaining attention on objectives despite temporary setbacks
- **Prepared Readiness:** Developing capabilities needed to receive desired outcomes

Your Manifestation Implementation Plan

- **Define specifically** what you want to achieve (vague wishes don't work)
- **Visualize regularly** as if you've already accomplished it
- **Align your actions** with your stated desires
- **Develop yourself** into someone capable of receiving it
- **Stay persistently focused** despite temporary obstacles

Call it manifestation, visualization, future-pacing, kumbaya, strategic planning—the process works when properly implemented. And in today's world, manifesting with intention works a lot faster—at 200 mph.

With genuine desire and appropriate action, you'll discover circumstances aligning to support your worthy aspirations.

Principle 26: **The Intentional Attraction System**

Create your desired future through clear visualization combined with aligned action. What you consistently focus on with genuine intention naturally manifests through your progressive transformation into someone capable of receiving it.

◎ Teach & Thrive

Here are five ways to develop manifestation skills in your children:

1. **Vision Board Evolution:** Create a traditional vision board, then make it actionable by adding the steps needed to get there. Create future boards that include not only desired outcomes but also required personal development and specific action steps. For younger children, use simple images and basic steps; for older children, develop sophisticated connections between desires and necessary actions.

2. **Identity Rehearsal Practice:** Help children practice being their future selves through visualization and action. Create regular "Future Self Sessions" where they mentally inhabit desired future states, experiencing associated emotions, thought patterns, and behaviors. Follow visualization with specific actions aligned with this future identity. For example, after visualizing themselves as responsible leaders, they might organize family activities that demonstrate those qualities.

3. **Opportunity Recognition Training:** Help children notice relevant opportunities through focused attention exercises. Encourage children to identify resources, connections, or information related to their goals within everyday experiences. Help them practice asking for what they

want firmly while identifying steps they could take to achieve it. My husband and I do this with the kids at every chance.

4. **Manifestation Evidence Collection:** Help children build belief in manifestation principles by pointing out real examples. Include both personal experiences and examples from others, creating a repository of evidence that reinforces the validity of these principles. Help them recognize that manifestation requires both asking clearly and taking consistent action toward their goals to produce desired results.

5. **Aligned Action Linking:** Help children understand the connections between daily choices and desired outcomes. Create "Dream-to-Daily" charts that show how specific, regular actions connect to ultimate goals. For example, linking how consistent reading practice connects to becoming an author, or how saving patterns relate to future financial freedom (to a vacation, to a better toy). This shows them that dreams require daily actions that connect where they are now to where they want to be.

Goal: Teach children to create their desired futures through clear visualization combined with aligned action—understanding that manifestation is about becoming who they need to be to achieve what they want.

Formula for Success

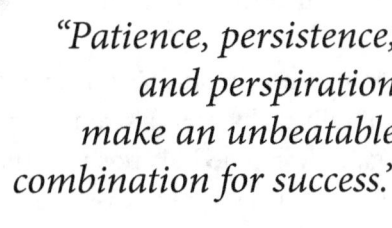

*"Patience, persistence,
and perspiration
make an unbeatable
combination for success."*

—Napoleon Hill

It's an open secret formula for success, but not many people practice it—the secret lies in consistently applying fundamental principles. The essential ingredients for any significant achievement are remarkably straightforward: identify WHAT you want, WANT it intensely, and DO what's necessary through focused action.

The Universal Success Formula = Desire + Clarity + Positive Habits + Intentional Action + Unwavering Discipline + Persistent Consistency

My Brother's 24-Year Medical Marathon

Let me illustrate this formula through my brother's extraordinary medical journey—a masterclass in consistency and persistence that would make marathon runners quit.

Despite exceptional academic performance, my brother struggled with interpersonal dynamics during his anesthesiology residency. After three years of dedicated work, organizational politics forced his withdrawal from the program. (Mom almost had those bragging rights. But he got on the black sheep list.)

Most people would have given up. My brother doubled down.

Without clear guidance but determined to continue, he obtained a master's degree and conducted research to strengthen his credentials for another residency application. Six years later, he secured a neurology residency position at the University of Texas in Houston.

Unfortunately, similar interpersonal challenges emerged. Despite his attending physician's strong support, conflicts with other staff members again threatened his position (had he learned the art of diplomacy, as Principle 16 suggests). Before contract expiration, the program director suggested transferring to internal medicine—a viable continuation path, a specialty potentially better aligned with his personality.

Here's where it gets interesting: his determination to specialize in higher-prestige fields led him to decline the transfer, resulting in contract expiration without completion.

Out of residency again. With substantial debt accumulated and twenty-four years invested, at age forty-two, his path forward seemed dark and exhausting. Most people would completely reconsider their life direction.

Not my brother. The formula continued working.

At a social gathering, my parents met a physician who offered valuable guidance. With this mentor's advice, my brother secured medical licenses in multiple states and identified suitable positions that leveraged his extensive education, despite his unconventional path.

His accumulated experience—combining two partial residencies, a master's degree, and extensive research—exceeded typical recent graduate qualifications. He ultimately secured a position as a physician with the

Department of Defense's medical department. He has received two promotions since then. Escaped the black sheep list. Whew!

This journey exemplifies focus, discipline, determination, and consistency—continuing pursuit despite extraordinary obstacles until the desired outcome is achieved.

But it's crucial to extract what made his journey unnecessarily more complicated—his missing ingredient was positive habits, especially people skills. We want to learn from others' mistakes (the cheapest lesson, Principle 19) because this gap made his journey longer, more agonizing, and more chaotic.

Achieving success and financial freedom is not easy, but absolutely possible with desire, clarity, intentional action, and persistence. The difference between "hard" and "unnecessarily brutal" comes down to having all the components working for you: the proper habits, strong foundation, and yes—the ability to work well with other people. That missing piece turned what could have been a challenging but manageable 8-year journey into a grueling 24-year marathon filled with politics, setbacks, and constant chaos.

Your journey's difficulty level, stress amount, and timeline depend heavily on whether you're building on solid fundamentals or constantly fighting upstream because of what you're missing.

The Success Formula Breakdown

- **WHAT (Clarity):** Know precisely what you seek. Not "have a good job", but "be a medical doctor, specializing in neurology." Not "make money" but "earn $100,000 annually or $200,000, or $2,000,000." Not "be successful" but "be a multi-millionaire with a net worth of $10,000,000."

- **WANT (Intensity):** Develop a genuine desire strong enough to sustain effort through inevitable challenges. My brother's medical obsession began in childhood through constant exposure to achievement discussions.

- **DO (Action):** Transform knowledge into immediate implementation. Every class my brother took, every activity he pursued, every decision he made served his medical goal.

- **Habits (Systems):** Establish behavioral patterns naturally generating progress. My brother maintained straight A's throughout school because academic excellence became his identity. However, he also has numerous other harmful habits that have contributed to many challenges in his journey.

- **Discipline (Consistency):** Continue necessary actions regardless of temporary fluctuations in motivation. When setbacks occurred, my brother found alternative paths rather than abandoning his objective.

- **Persistence (Determination):** Maintain course despite obstacles, setbacks, or apparent failures. "Never retreat in battle" means continuing until you achieve your objective, regardless of temporary circumstances. "Always finish what you start!"

The Universal Application

This formula works across all domains:

- **Financial goals:** Clear targets, genuine desire, consistent investing habits, disciplined spending, persistent accumulation
- **Health objectives:** Specific fitness goals, motivated commitment, daily exercise habits, nutritional discipline, long-term consistency
- **Relationship success:** Clear relationship values, genuine commitment, positive interaction habits, conflict resolution discipline, persistent investment

Your Success Formula Implementation

1. **Define your WHAT** with specific, measurable clarity
2. **Strengthen your WANT** by connecting to deeper motivations
3. **Design your DO** through systematic daily actions
4. **Install supporting HABITS** that naturally generate progress
5. **Build DISCIPLINE** to continue when motivation fluctuates
6. **Commit to PERSISTENCE** regardless of temporary setbacks

> **The universe often presents unexpected opportunities to those who demonstrate sufficient determination.**

The Universe is on your side if you want it enough. Whether pursuing a medical specialization, financial independence, or any significant objective, fundamental principles remain consistent: clearly identify your goal, intensely desire it, and persistently take appropriate action until success is achieved.

Now, how quickly you can get there and how quickly the Universe can help you depend on your habits and other preparations. Success timeframes vary significantly depending on individual circumstances, but mastering these fundamental Principles in this book dramatically accelerates progress. The disciplined habits, positive self-image, and unwavering confidence developed through previous principles create the foundation supporting consistent action toward your objective.

Believe in your deservingness, maintain confidence in your capability, express gratitude for progress, celebrate meaningful milestones (without excess), and continuously improve your approach.

Principle 27: **The Universal Achievement Formula**

Success follows a consistent pattern, regardless of the domain: clearly identify your objective, genuinely desire its attainment, and persistently implement the necessary actions despite temporary obstacles or setbacks.

◎ Teach & Thrive

Here are five ways to develop achievement skills in your children:

1. **SMART Goal Progression:** Teach your children to set SMART goals: Specific, Measurable, Achievable, Relevant, and Time-bound. Create age-appropriate "Goal Building Blocks" that develop each part step by step. For younger children, focus on specificity and measurement; for older children, incorporate all five elements with increasing sophistication. Document goals, tracking progress, and celebrating milestones.

2. **Desire Development:** Strengthen children's emotional connections to their goals. Create "Why Power" exercises that progressively drill deeper. Begin with surface reasons, then guide them through at least five progressively deeper "why" questions, uncovering core motivations. Create visual or tangible representations of these deeper motivations for daily reinforcement.

3. **Intention-to-Action Training:** Convert intentions into actions through a specific planning methodology. Teach "When-Then" frameworks, where each goal-supporting behavior receives concrete implementation parameters. Instead of "I'll practice piano more," establish "When I finish homework each day, then I'll practice piano

for 20 minutes in the living room before any play time." Document these intentions and track completion.

4. **Obstacle Premortem Practice:** Develop children's resilience by systematically anticipating and preparing for challenges. Before beginning significant goals, conduct planning sessions where they identify potential obstacles and develop specific contingency plans for each. Create visual "If-Then Scenarios" showing predetermined responses to common setbacks. This teaches them to plan ahead for problems instead of giving up when challenges appear. "What will you do if this happens?"

5. **Consistency Reinforcement System:** Strengthen children's ability to maintain action through visual tracking. Create "Consistency Chains" where each day of goal-supporting behavior adds a visible link. Help them connect cause and effect. For example, Max made this connection: "I went to bed early, I had energy in class, and I paid attention and did all my work. So now I have less homework." He got the point. This builds understanding that consistent small actions create compounding results.

Goal: Develop children who understand that success follows predictable patterns and who can systematically apply these patterns to achieve their most important objectives.

Take the Bullet Train

"If I have seen further, it is by standing on the shoulders of giants."

—*Sir Isaac Newton*

You can reach your destination via two public transportation options: the local bus with frequent stops, or the high-speed bullet train that delivers you directly to the success station.

The bullet train requires greater initial investment but provides exponential time savings and dramatically better results.

The Mentorship Acceleration Advantage

The fastest route to success involves finding proven experts and following established pathways. While you can certainly succeed through independent exploration (and many do), having qualified mentorship dramatically accelerates progress by helping you bypass common pitfalls and implement proven strategies.

I understood the importance of mentorship early, but regretted not pursuing this advantage more aggressively. While I had inspiring role models, I lacked direct guidance from someone who could provide personalized direction, and this was the link that could have set me FURTHER and help me arrive SOONER.

Johnny's Credit Card Investment Strategy

My husband exemplifies purchasing acceleration perfectly. When we first dated, he was spectacularly broke—not "struggling artist" broke, but "maxing out multiple credit cards to afford a $10,000 training program" broke.

(Pro tip: You know someone's financial situation by their credit limits. He needed multiple cards because each had pathetic limits. Meanwhile, I could put a down payment for a house on my credit card, or buy a car in full.)

Despite lacking savings, Johnny identified high-income skills and invested in specialized SEO training from industry leaders. The program cost more than his entire net worth, but he viewed it as an investment in his education rather than an expense.

He immersed himself completely, studying day and night to rapidly develop his expertise.

But technical capability alone proved insufficient. He needed clients to monetize these skills. Recognizing this gap, he invested in Grant Cardone's sales training (before Cardone achieved billionaire status and shifted focus to real estate education).

He subsequently added Dan Lok's high-ticket closing program and other specialized training.

These strategic investments allowed him to "stand on the shoulders of giants"—leveraging accumulated wisdom to implement proven systems immediately rather than spending years discovering practical approaches through trial and error.

My Real Estate Mentorship Discovery

For my real estate journey, I knew WHAT I wanted (property investment) but initially lacked clarity about HOW to begin. IBM unexpectedly provided this missing link by connecting me with colleagues already implementing successful strategies.

During orientation, I met a remarkable 23-year-old who owned rental property and came from a family of successful investors. His parents had retired early, earning a substantial passive income from their portfolio.

Through IBM, I encountered numerous colleagues investing in real estate, including another 23-year-old who owned multiple single-family rentals. He generously shared his approach, including specific market selection criteria and investment strategies. He essentially convinced and nudged me to acquire properties. I didn't even know how to underwrite or do any calculation; I just dove right in. Fortunately, the calculation was very simple: rent needed to be more than the monthly mortgage, and that was very easy back then.

This guidance directed my focus to purchase in the same markets where he was building his portfolio. I acquired my first property at 26 and a second within a year. He had turned 24 at this point, and I just turned 26. He said, "Not bad for 26."

Then he continued, "Yesterday you were a beauty, now you're 26 and it's all going downhill from here." And there it was—the reminder that youth doesn't last forever. Twenty-six felt different. No longer the early 20s, where time feels infinite. Now the clock was ticking, and I could hear it. Twenty-six had become my personal midlife crisis—except instead of buying a convertible, I was calculating compound interest.

Opportunities in Economic Disruptions

2008 Housing Market Correction

I missed significant opportunities due to a lack of knowledge and inadequate mentorship. That period represented one of the most significant wealth-transfer opportunities in modern history.

I was on track to acquire two properties a year, at least that was my plan. I got one under contract for $200K with a value over $300K (now worth well over $600,000), but I operated on emotion (avoid by mastering Principle 18) and backed out the week of closing. With proper guidance, I could have acquired numerous distressed properties at exceptional valuations.

Since 2008, we've witnessed another major economic disruption:

COVID-19 Pandemic (2020)

The market crash created exceptional buying opportunities. Stocks like energy, oil and gas, airlines, and GE plummeted—the perfect moment to double down for those with conviction. I made some money but didn't go all-in because I'm not a huge risk-taker by nature.

Here's the truth: **You can achieve financial freedom without taking extreme risks.** But if you want to get super rich, you need the conviction to make bold moves and take big risks.

Major economic disruptions create extraordinary opportunities for those prepared to recognize and act on them.

In a typical lifetime, if you're fortunate, you might witness two such pivotal moments. Proper preparation for these moments can help you seize opportunities you would otherwise miss, without even realizing it.

*"Success is where preparation
and opportunity meet."*

—Bobby Unser

Consider this: praying for rain means nothing without a vessel to catch it. When opportunity pours down like gold coins, only those with buckets positioned can collect the wealth. The rest watch fortune fall past them.

Mentorship Acquisition Strategy

Identify potential mentors by evaluating:

- **Proven results** in your area of interest
- **Teaching ability** and willingness to share knowledge
- **Value alignment** with your principles and approach
- **Accessibility** through direct contact or educational programs

Maximize mentorship value through:

- **Prepared questions** that demonstrate a serious commitment
- **Implemented action** on guidance received
- **Respectful appreciation** for time and wisdom shared
- **Documented learning** to reinforce and review insights

The Investment Perspective

View mentorship as your highest-return investment:

- **Time savings** from avoiding common mistakes
- **Opportunity identification** through experienced guidance

- **Strategy refinement** based on proven approaches
- **Network access** through mentor connections
- **Confidence-building** through expert validation

Your Bullet Train Boarding Pass

This week, identify one area where mentorship could accelerate your progress:

- Research those who have achieved the results you want
- Determine how to access their guidance (programs, books, direct contact)
- Prepare specific questions demonstrating a serious commitment
- Take immediate action on any guidance received

Remember: The first step toward any achievement is knowing *what* you want; the *how* follows naturally with sufficient commitment. If you genuinely pursue your objective with determination, the necessary resources and methodologies will emerge through unexpected channels. You can also seek guidance from those who've already successfully traveled the path.

Principle 28: **The Mentor Acceleration System**

Dramatically accelerate your progress by following proven pathways. Rather than reinventing processes through costly trial and error, leverage accumulated wisdom from those who have already achieved your objectives.

◎ Teach & Thrive

Here are five ways to develop mentor utilization skills in your children:

1. **Mentor Identification Guide:** Create a questions template: "Has this person achieved what I want to achieve?" "Do they teach others effectively?" "Do their values align with mine?" Guide children through evaluating potential mentors against these criteria. This teaches them how to discern qualified guidance from merely accessible advice.

2. **Learning Extraction System:** Maximize value from mentorship interactions by creating a "Mentor Meeting List" with three phases: Before (preparing specific questions and objectives), During (active listening and documentation), and After (implementation planning and follow-up questions). Practice this system with family members before applying to external mentors.

3. **Pattern Recognition Training:** Help children spot proven pathways in different areas. Create examples of achievement in their areas of interest. Guide them to identify common elements, prerequisite skills, and frequent obstacles across these examples. This builds the ability to recognize established pathways.

4. **Implementation Acceleration Protocol:** Teach children to convert knowledge into action—quickly implement rather than wait for perfect understanding; do-then-improve. This teaches them to learn by doing instead of waiting until they know everything.

5. **Mentor Network Development:** Help children build relationships with mentors appropriate to their age and interests. Start with accessible people: family members, friends' parents or parents' friends. Progress to community experts: local business owners, professionals in fields of interest. Eventually introduce industry leaders through events or networking.

Goal: Develop children who naturally stand on the shoulders of giants—learning from those who've already achieved what they aspire to accomplish.

If You Don't Have This, You Won't Get It

"He who has a why to live can bear almost any how."

—*Friedrich Nietzsche*

Maintain laser focus on your objectives and clearly understand your fundamental motivations. If you lack clarity about your destination and compelling reasons for pursuing it, you'll likely abandon your journey when inevitable challenges arise.

Your "why" must be stronger than your "why not."

The Internal Conflict Problem

Why do you want to increase your income? Why do you want millionaire status? Why do you desire financial freedom?

If you harbor internal conflicts, such as "I don't really need a lot of money" or "Money can't buy happiness," you'll subconsciously undermine your own progress.

The cycle goes like this, and it leads you to nowhere: When you struggle to book a nice hotel for your family, you remember that you do need money. Or when your kids want to participate in an extracurricular activity that you don't have the money for, you wish you had more money. But all other days, when you don't want to wake up early for work or stay up late to learn a skill (but binge on Netflix instead), you convince yourself that you don't need money. And that's how most people stay where they are.

> **You can't successfully pursue what you don't believe you deserve or what conflicts with your core values.**

My Fundamental WHY

When financial goals become challenging, I reconnect with my core motivations:

Primary Motivation: My children. Giving them a great life—high-quality experiences, real opportunities, access and privileges. The financial freedom to live on my terms, to have more time with them, and create exceptional memories together while continuously opening new doors for their future.

Secondary Motivations:

- Enjoying life's highest quality offerings rather than settling for compromised alternatives
- Building intergenerational wealth that benefits future generations
- Creating positive impact through the resources I develop
- Having the freedom to be generous

The Language of Commitment

Notice the difference between tentative and committed language:

- **Tentative:** "I'll try to save more money" / "I hope to start investing" / "Maybe I can build a business"
- **Committed:** "I will save 50% of my income" / "I must achieve financial independence by 40" / "I am building multiple income streams"

Always remember your fundamental WHY and maintain an uncompromising commitment, expressed through "I must" and "I will," rather than tentative language like "I'll try" or "I hope to."

The Clarity-Persistence Connection

The clarity and intensity of your motivation directly determine your persistence when facing challenges. Those with compelling, emotionally resonant reasons for achieving financial independence consistently outperform those with merely an intellectual understanding of its benefits.

Consider these motivation levels:

- **Weak:** "It would be nice to have more money."
- **Moderate:** "I want financial security."
- **Strong:** "I must achieve financial independence."
- **Unshakeable:** "I *will* create generational wealth that transforms my family's trajectory forever to give my children a fun-filled life with privileges and opportunities."

The WHY Depth Assessment

Test your motivations with progressive questioning:

- Why do you want financial freedom?
- Why does that matter to you?
- What would that enable you to do or become?
- How would that change your family's future?

- What legacy would that create?

Continue until you reach emotional core motivations that generate energy rather than drain it. Ask "Why" until you have goosebumps and then tears. (Don't ask me why unless you bring a box of tissues and have a joke to pull me out of it.)

My Deepest Motivation

I have many Why's, but my deepest motivation is my kids. Whenever I'm tempted to settle for "good enough", I remind myself that my children's future depends on the actions I take today.

I want to give them a head start—to achieve more than I have and build upon the foundation I'm creating. More importantly, I want to equip them to work strategically in their teens, 20s, and 30s—so their 40s and beyond can focus on enjoying life's finest offerings and making a meaningful impact. This vision drives every financial decision I make.

When I'm tempted to spend on immediate gratification, I remember: every dollar invested now creates more options for my children's future. Every sacrifice today becomes our advantage tomorrow.

Your WHY Development Challenge

This week, clarify and strengthen your fundamental motivations:

1. **Identify your core reasons** for pursuing financial success
2. **Connect emotionally** with how achievement would transform your life and others'
3. **Articulate specific outcomes** you want to create or prevent
4. **Document your WHY** in compelling, emotional language
5. **Review regularly,** especially when motivation wavers

Create a written statement beginning with "I must and I will achieve financial independence because..."

Make it so compelling that reading it immediately rekindles your motivation, regardless of your current circumstances.

Remember: Clarity of purpose plus intensity of desire equals unstoppable determination.

When your "why" is clear and compelling, the "how" becomes secondary. You'll find ways to overcome obstacles because giving up simply isn't an option.

Principle 29: **The Motivational Clarity Principle**

Clearly identify your ultimate objectives and develop emotionally compelling reasons for their achievement. Your ability to persist through challenges directly correlates with the clarity and power of your fundamental motivations.

◎ Teach & Thrive

Here are five ways to develop motivational clarity in your children:

1. **Motivational Depth Exploration:** Improve goal-setting by asking deeper and deeper "Why" questions. Create exercises where they identify initial reasons for goals, then systematically explore deeper motivations with "Why does that matter?" questions. Continue this process through at least five levels until you reach the core emotional drivers.

2. **Purpose Connection Linking:** Help children connect daily actions to ultimate goals through visual links. Create "Purpose Pathways" that show how specific daily behaviors directly connect to meaningful long-term outcomes. For younger children, use simple illustrations; for older children, develop sophisticated connection diagrams. Review these regularly.

3. **Contrast Motivation Training:** Build emotional commitment by having children compare different possible futures. Create "Two Paths" visualization exercises that allow them to experience both the desired outcomes of persistent effort and the potential consequences of abandoning pursuits. Make these experiences multi-sensory and

emotionally resonant rather than merely intellectual. This builds motivational clarity by showing them what they're choosing between.

4. **Language Practice:** Build children's use of commitment language— showing them how word choice affects determination. Replace tentative phrases ("I'll try" or "I hope to") with commitment statements ("I will" or "I must"). Create "Power Words" lists for their goals. Practice these new linguistic patterns through role-play until they become natural expressions.

5. **Motivation Renewal Rituals:** Create regular practices for reconnecting with core motivations. Create "Purpose Refresh" protocols with specific steps, including reviewing the deepest motivations, reconnecting with emotional drivers, and visualizing successful completion. Implement this protocol whenever motivation wanes. This teaches self-motivation instead of depending on external encouragement.

Goal: Help children develop such clear, compelling reasons for their goals that persistence becomes automatic rather than forced—creating internal motivation that sustains effort through any challenge.

PRINCIPLE 30

Roadmap to Getting RICH

> *"It's not how much money you make,*
> *but how much money you keep,*
> *how hard it works for you, and how many generations you*
> *keep it for."*

—*Robert Kiyosaki*

The fundamental pathway to financial independence remains remarkably consistent across time and circumstances—a tale as old as commerce itself, yet frequently overlooked in pursuit of shortcuts or novelty.

The wealth-building recipe is simple: make good money, save aggressively, invest in assets that produce income, and repeat.

Investment Lesson From Max

One day, while I was driving the kids to Taekwondo class, Max asked, "Mama, do you know what 'investing' is?"

I curiously asked, "What is it?"

Max explained: "Investing is when you go to sleep and when you wake up, your money doubles."

"Wow! What a good investment," I said.

Max continued: "It's like you have $100, and the next day, you have $200."

The kid got it.

The Wealth-Building Framework

Step 1: Master High-Income Skills. Develop capabilities that generate substantial market value, either through self-employment or organizational roles. Select skills with strong demand, significant compensation, and sustainable positioning. Become a subject matter expert and dominate. (Refer to Principle 24)

Step 2: Generate High-Income Earnings. Monetize your expertise effectively. This might mean climbing corporate ladders, building businesses, or creating multiple income streams.

Step 3: Implement Aggressive Saving. Ideally, save 50% or more of earnings. The more you earn, the higher the percentage you should save. When you can live comfortably on 10-20% of your income, you know you're winning.

Step 4: Invest in Income-Producing Assets. Purchase assets that generate cash flow: rental properties, dividend stocks, businesses, or other investments that pay you regularly.

Step 5: Diversify Income Streams. Never depend on a single income source. Build multiple revenue streams, including passive income.

Step 6: Repeat the Cycle. Continuously acquire, accumulate, and amass assets that generate more income for additional investment.

Collect A's to Get F's

Not the A's from school—straight A's alone won't make you rich. The A's that actually build wealth: Acquire, Accumulate, and Amass Assets. These are what lead to the F's worth chasing: F.U. Money, Financial Freedom, and the freedom of time, location, and choice.

With a strong foundation built in Part 1 and proper conditioning from Principle 9 (collecting mindset) and Principle 27 (formula for success), this accumulation approach becomes natural rather than requiring constant discipline.

My Chosen Vehicle

Armed with confidence, skills, proper conditioning, stacked on top of strong habits, along with unshakeable determination, you can choose any vehicle to reach financial freedom. I chose project management for enterprise software companies managing large-scale implementations.

The logic was simple: substantial income requires working on high-value projects that generate significant revenue.

Let's make it crystal clear: the salary of an office assistant at a small non-profit differs drastically from that of an assistant to the CEO of a Fortune 500 company. A real estate agent selling $200,000 homes earns far less than one who closes $2 million properties. A project manager overseeing $10,000 hospitality projects receives a fraction of what a PM managing $100 million software implementations commands.

Companies can't pay you hundreds of thousands of dollars if the project you work on only generates a few thousand.

It doesn't matter how hard you work or how many hours you log—what matters is the revenue your effort generates.

My chosen skills and areas of focus are project management and real estate—both involve working on high-value projects and substantial deals. You can select any high-income skill in any field. It doesn't have to be a doctor or a lawyer. Sales, digital marketing, consulting, specialized tech skills—choose something that interests you, that you're naturally good at, and that *pays* well.

If you don't have money to save and it's not a spending-habit issue, it's a skill issue. The first step is developing high-income skills that increase your earning capacity and savings.

Before you start with the "but I can't" excuses—I've witnessed it with my own two eyes. My husband transformed from working two jobs to building his own business by investing in himself to acquire high-income skills, even when he was so broke that he had to split the training costs across multiple credit cards. If he can transition from working two low-paying jobs to building a profitable business, anyone willing to invest in acquiring high-income skills can do the same.

The Wealth Reality Check

Let's be clear: getting rich isn't about monetary accumulation but instead securing the freedoms money enables—financial security, quality experiences, time autonomy, and purposeful impact.

The goal is to collect assets that generate enough passive income to cover your desired lifestyle without financial stress and requiring you to trade your time until 70.

Roadmap to wealth is an open secret that many don't apply = High-income skill → High-income earning → Save to invest → Acquire income-producing assets → Create multiple income sources → Repeat.

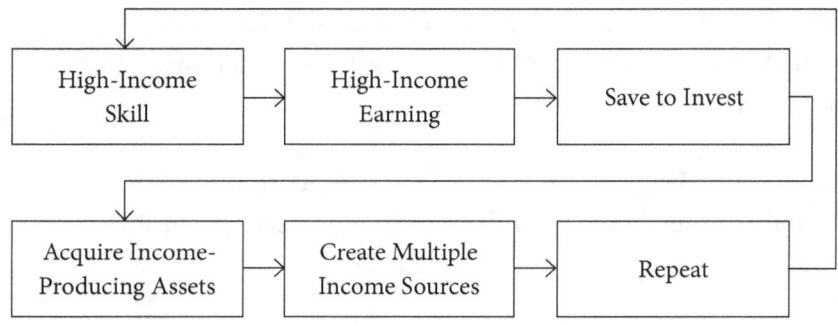

Countless financially successful people have proved it. **It works! You just need to apply it.**

Levels of Financial Freedom & F.U. Number

You need to figure out your F.U. number to have a clear goal and target. Calculate it by adding up the cost to sustain your current lifestyle—or the lifestyle you desire. Dan Lok discusses this concept in his book *F.U. Money*. F.U. stands for... well, you know what.

Actually, in this context, F.U. stands for **Freedom Upgrade**. Your Freedom Upgrade number is the amount of passive income that allows you to live the lifestyle you want without reporting to a 9-to-5 or trading your time for money.

What F.U. number—and what level of financial freedom—would give you the freedom you need?

F.U. Levels

F.U. Level 1: Independent—Free from the 9-to-5 job. Your passive income covers your current lifestyle without requiring active work.

F.U. Level 2: High-Net-Worth ($1M–$10M)—Quality lifestyle with access to premium experiences, expanded opportunities, and meaningful privileges. Ability to pursue significant goals.

F.U. Level 3: Very High Net Worth / Abundance ($10M–$50M)— Freedom of choice. Higher quality lifestyle with access to most premium experiences, opportunities, and privileges.

F.U. Level 4: Ultra High Net Worth / Ultimate Freedom ($50M–$500M)—Substantial wealth that provides nearly unlimited options and access to the most exclusive experiences.

F.U. Level 5: Indestructible Rich ($500M–$10B)—Generational wealth that can withstand almost anything.

F.U. Level 6: Titan ($10B+)—Elon Musk territory. Resources comparable to nation-states. The absolute apex of personal wealth.

The truth is: You don't need to reach Level 4 to achieve financial freedom. Most of us can provide our families with extraordinary lives filled with opportunities and live entirely on our own terms at Level 1 or 2.

But here's my advice: aim for Level 3 or 4. That way, God forbid, if you fall short, you'll land at Level 2—and still be living an incredible life.

Your Wealth Construction Action Plan

1. **Assess current position**: What's your income, savings rate, and asset base?
2. **Identify skill gaps**: What capabilities would increase your earning potential?
3. **Optimize savings rate**: How much can you realistically save monthly?
4. **Research investment options**: Which assets align with your risk tolerance and timeline?
5. **Create a timeline**: When do you want to achieve financial independence?

Start where you are, use what you have, do what you can.

> The path to wealth isn't mysterious or exclusive—it's systematic and available to anyone willing to apply these proven principles consistently over time.

The Children's Head Start Program

For parents seeking to give children financial advantages, consider these strategic approaches:

Foundation Building:

- Establish early savings vehicles, maximizing compound growth
- Open tax-advantaged 529 education plans
- Create custodial accounts (UTMA/UGMA) for asset holdings
- Consider whole life insurance with cash value (This is what my parents established for all of us, and it's proven invaluable)

Education Implementation:

- Teach investment principles through small stock positions that they can track
- Develop financial literacy through age-appropriate budgeting activities
- Establish family banking systems where children can borrow and repay with interest

Advanced Strategies:

- Help older children establish credit histories through monitored accounts
- Consider insurance strategies to develop financial safety nets
- Explore trust structures for long-term asset protection
- Encourage entrepreneurial initiatives to develop commercial thinking—put them to work early (and no, it's not child abuse or

stealing their childhood). Make it fun: dog walking for neighbors, pet sitting, lemonade stands in summer, hot chocolate in winter

Principle 30: **The Wealth Construction Blueprint**

Follow proven wealth-building progressions through skill development, income generation, disciplined saving, and strategic asset acquisition. This timeless approach consistently produces financial independence when implemented with patience and persistence.

◎ Teach & Thrive

Here are five ways to develop wealth-building skills in your children:

1. **Money Growth Visualization:** For younger children, create "Money Gardens" and "Money Jar" where physical objects represent initial investments and money grows. For older children, develop interactive spreadsheets or visual simulations showing how money multiplies over time with consistent additions and growth rates.

2. **Asset Identification Training:** Teach children to tell the difference between assets and liabilities. Create "Asset Detective" games where they evaluate various purchases based on whether they: 1) Increase in value, 2) generate income, or 3) decrease in value and create expenses. Use examples relevant to their experience, gradually increasing sophistication as they mature.

3. **Income Skill Development Framework:** Help children identify and develop high-value capabilities. Create "Income Superpower" programs where they explore valuable skills, choose ones that match their interests and strengths, and then build mastery through focused practice.

4. **Saving System:** Establish age-appropriate frameworks for systematic saving that foster lifelong savings habits. Develop "Three-Jar Methods" (or digital equivalents) that automatically divide income among Spending, Saving, and Sharing categories before consumption decisions are made. This builds automatic saving habits preceding all successful investing.

5. **Financial Independence Roadmap:** Help children understand the complete wealth-building path. Design "Freedom Journey" boards showing sequential stages from skill development through asset acquisition to financial independence. Establish clear milestones marking progress along this continuum, celebrating achievements at each stage. This shows them that wealth creation follows clear, predictable steps.

Goal: Install understanding that wealth building follows predictable patterns that anyone can learn and apply, combined with practical skills to begin implementing these patterns immediately.

PRINCIPLE 31

Front-Load

*"You may delay,
but time will not."*

—*Benjamin Franklin*

Always front-load effort and tackle the most challenging aspects first.
This approach fundamentally differs from academic test-taking strategies,
which recommend tackling the easiest questions first to maximize points
within time constraints.

**In the broader context of life, confronting difficult challenges initially
yields superior results.**

The Energy Management Reality

Significant challenges typically require greater energy and focus—
resources that diminish throughout the day. By addressing demanding
tasks initially, you resolve major issues while your capabilities remain at
peak levels.

**My front-loading strategy applies to everything: work projects, travel
itineraries, and even household responsibilities.**

When traveling to multiple destinations, I start with the farthest or most challenging location and work my way progressively toward easier, more familiar territory. When organizing events, I secure the most critical elements first (venues, key participants, core resources) before addressing secondary details.

The Academic vs. Life Principle Inversion

Most educational approaches actually teach patterns opposite to life's optimal strategies. Recognizing which academic principles require inversion for real-world application represents essential discernment.

- **Academic Strategy:** Do easy problems first to maximize points within time limits
- **Life Strategy:** Do hard tasks first while energy and focus remain strongest
- **Academic Strategy:** Don't copy others' work
- **Life Strategy:** Model successful approaches (Amazon adapted eBay's marketplace concept)

Rushing and Procrastination Are Both Detrimental

Procrastination represents one of the most destructive habits that can hinder achievement—delaying until deadlines creates pressure, stress, and compromised quality or missed opportunities. However, rushing to react is no better than procrastination. Taking immediate actions sounds like the opposite of procrastination, but without reviewing the process or weighing options, it often leads to negative results.

The habit of doing things without thinking, which frequently causes rework, stems from rushing. The cost of constantly reworking is time and resources.

While we don't want to procrastinate, we don't want to rush either. Rushing doesn't mean fast when the result needs to be redone. *Efficiency* is performing tasks correctly and quickly through appropriate methodology and strategic sequencing.

The Bicycle Paint Disaster

Max wanted to repaint his bicycle before the spring weather allowed him to ride. If he procrastinated, he'd miss the best cycling months.

Max picked his favorite spray paint color at Home Depot, but in their rush, they grabbed the wrong type. He and my husband, excitedly, started spraying, skipping crucial prep steps—no surface preparation, wrong paint formula. The paint rubbed off as soon as it dried.

What should have been a weekend project turned into weeks of painstakingly scraping off failed paint. The lesson: doing it right the first time is faster than both rushing and procrastinating.

If you find yourself constantly having to do things twice or rework projects, it's a sign you have a rushing habit and need to adjust your approach.

The Life Application Philosophy

If you don't work when you're young, you will have to work harder when you're old.

One night while we were getting ready for bed, Max told me, "Daddy did not work when he was young, so now he has to work harder and doesn't have time to play with us. You have to work hard when you're young so you can play more when you grow up." Out of the mouths of babes—Max had grasped the fundamental principle. This concept applies universally—complete homework before recreational activities

Handle essential responsibilities before enjoyable pursuits

Work and invest aggressively during your 20s and 30s rather than delaying until later decades

> **Early financial discipline creates the option to enjoy prosperity during your most physically capable years—rather than achieving comfort only when health may limit your ability to enjoy it.**

The Seasons of Life Strategy

Tony Robbins conceptualizes life stages as seasons: Spring (ages 1-20), Summer (ages 21-41), Fall (ages 42-62), and Winter (ages 63+). When you plant the right seeds and nurture them during Spring and Summer, you harvest in Fall with sufficient reserves for Winter.

Most People's Season of Life:

Spring (ages 1-20): Learning and growing

Summer (21-41): More school, slacking off, indulging, working just to get by

Fall (42-62): Playing catch-up, working harder

Winter (63+): Still working

Late Winter (67+): Finally retire with the bare minimum

Our Acceleration to Freedom:

Spring (ages 1-15): Learning and growing

Summer (16-39): Learning AND working. Yes, work! Kids can start working as early as twelve or even ten, taking on responsibilities in exchange for money. Work double. Work extra. Work as much as humanly possible in your teens, 20s, and 30s. Save aggressively and invest strategically.

Fall (40-62): Enjoying accumulated wealth. Live FREELY. Forty is when life truly begins. The goal is to achieve financial freedom before 40.

Winter (63+): Enjoying accrued wealth. Live FREELY.

Why wait until 67?

The Dream Car Question

Would you rather drive your Lambo—or whatever your dream car is—when you're 30 or 60?

The reality is, when people finally get their dream car later in life, it's never as thrilling as it would have been when they were younger. It's like finally getting that bike you wanted as a kid—but you're thirty now. It's just not the same.

I'm not a car enthusiast, but I do appreciate nice things (and I admit it). That luxurious Mercedes finally became a reality for me, and I love my G-Wagon—which, let's be real, is a significant upgrade from those '90s Mercedes sedans with their iconic hood ornaments. Plus, the massive trunk can fit four more people.

But I wish I'd reached this milestone in my early 30s, or even my 20s. Let's be honest: driving your dream car in your 20s or 30s is far more enjoyable than finally getting it in your 60s. This isn't just about the car—it's about achieving your goals earlier. Achieving financial freedom earlier means enjoying its benefits during your most energetic, vital years—for decades longer.

Your Front-Loading Implementation Strategy

Daily Level:

- Handle most challenging tasks during peak energy periods
- Complete important work before checking email or social media
- Address potential problems before they become urgent crises

Project Level:

- Secure critical resources and commitments first
- Build buffer time for unexpected complications
- Front-load research and planning phases

Life Level:

- Invest heavily in skills and assets during the early years
- Create systems and passive income before you need them
- Build financial independence while YOUNG so you can enjoy SOONER than most

The Smooth Sailing Advantage

When you front-load effort, the end phases become progressively easier rather than increasingly stressful. This creates positive momentum and allows course corrections if necessary. Front-load your efforts on the financial freedom journey to get ahead—so that 40 and beyond can be smooth sailing, instead of struggling to catch up until you finally slow down at 70, when your body limits what you can enjoy.

Mind-Blowing Shift

I want to train my children to work twice as hard in their teens, 20s, and 30s—then enjoy the freedom most people never reach. Part of that strategy? Let them stay home while they build their foundation.

Both of my siblings and I stayed at home and attended the local university. Free rent. Free utilities. Free food. Free car. Free insurance. We saved everything we earned, which gave us a massive head start.

Now imagine a family with three or four working adult children, each contributing modestly to household expenses while saving aggressively. Everyone wins: parents have extra to invest, children build wealth early, and the family unit grows stronger financially—together.

Your Front-Loading Challenge

- This week, identify one area where you can apply front-loading:
- A project that would benefit from early difficult work
- A skill development objective that would benefit from early, intensive focus
- A financial goal that would benefit from early aggressive action

Remember: The sequence of effort often matters more than the total amount. Do the hard parts first, and everything else becomes easier.

Principle 31: **The Front-Loading Advantage**

Tackle your most challenging tasks first when your resources are at their strongest. Complete preparatory work before enjoyment and invest heavily during the early years for the maximum benefit period. This approach delivers superior results by appropriately sequencing effort.

◉ Teach & Thrive

Here are five ways to develop strategic sequencing skills in your children:

1. **Effort Sequencing Framework:** Train children to do the complex tasks first. Create "Challenge First" protocols where they identify the most difficult or essential elements before beginning, and prioritize from difficult to easy tasks. Practice this approach with increasingly complex activities, from homework assignments to longer-term projects.

2. **Identify High Energy Exercise:** Help children understand their personal energy patterns to optimize task scheduling. Guide them to identify and log focus, motivation, and effectiveness at different times of day and week. Use this information to find their best times for hard work.

3. **Front-Loading Simulation:** Develop children's appreciation for front-loaded effort. Demonstrate this through a game competition: Two rows of cups filled with water, lined up (make sure it's a long line of 30 cups). Each row has a bucket in the front. One kid starts in the front, and another kid starts at the end of the row. Use the timer to see who finishes dumping all the water from the cups into the bucket. The

demo has shown that the kid who starts in the back is faster and less tired at the end.

4. **Work-Before-Play Training:** Strengthen children's ability to complete necessary work before engaging in entertainment through gradual practice. Create "Work-Before-Play" list that specifies which responsibilities must be completed before various rewards.

5. **Front-Loading Life Strategy:** Help children understand how front-loading effort compounds over time by showing early versus late effort distributions. Start kids working early: lemonade stands, dog walking, lawn care, babysitting, pet sitting, car washing, house sitting at age 10-12; older kids, age 13-15: lifeguarding, camp counselor, tutoring, coaching youth sports. Early work builds savings, skills, and a work ethic simultaneously. Show the math: starting at twelve versus twenty-two creates decades of compound advantage.

Goal: Develop children who instinctively front-load effort—tackle challenging work first when their energy and resources are strongest, and start employment and invest aggressively early—understanding that strategic sequencing and early financial discipline create decades of freedom rather than a lifetime of playing catch-up.

Create Your Own Club

"Don't wait for opportunity.
Create it."

—*George Bernard Shaw*

Sometimes conventional inclusion isn't necessary or optimal. Rather than seeking acceptance from existing groups that require you to compromise your authenticity, consider creating your own communities aligned with your genuine values and vision.

In preschool, Max wanted to join two other boys during recess, but they consistently pushed him away and excluded him from activities. When I asked him who his favorite and least favorite person at school was today, he shared his challenge: "I have two favorites, but they don't want to play with me."

I asked, "Why do you want to play with them when you can play with other kids?" Max replied: "Because they are awesome."

I reassured him: "You're awesome too, you're the most awesome person I know. You can be friends with other kids and teach them to be awesome like you."

You don't need permission to be awesome. You just need to start being awesome and create your own club.

The Self-Authorization Revolution

Define what you consider "cool" without external validation. Establish your own standards of "fun" and invite compatible individuals to join—attract your own tribe. Rather than conforming to others' expectations, authorize yourself to create environments that reflect your authentic preferences.

This principle applies across personal, social, and professional domains.

From friendship circles to business ventures, the ability to create rather than merely join represents a fundamental distinction between leaders and followers.

This self-authorization approach connects to several earlier principles, particularly authentic validation (Principle 21) and association selection (Principle 14). Rather than discounting yourself to be on the same sales rack, create environments that attract those already aligned with your values and vision. This reverses the conventional approach of seeking acceptance through conformity.

My Revolution: Bar to Ballroom

Moving to the Washington, DC area without any family or friends, I was fortunate to share a small, modest cottage with two sweet and cool girls, a few Metro stops from the city. I wished bonding involved something other than pretending to like the rubbing alcohol mixed with the red-dyed solution masquerading as a cocktail.

I've always wanted to take ballroom dance lessons. But it was nearly impossible during college—registration required a dance partner, and finding a 20-year-old guy willing to ballroom dance in Baton Rouge was mission impossible.

Day two in DC, my mission was to find a ballroom studio. After trying several, I found one that became my second home. I traveled for work during the week, and when I returned on the weekends, I spent every waking moment dancing—igniting my soul instead of burying it, pretending to be "normal," and suffering from bar-hopping.

The Childhood Social Tribe

Most children face social challenges that require either conformity to groups that don't align with their values or complete isolation from social connections. Adults face this too.

There's a third option: creating environments based on their authentic interests.

Instead of desperately pursuing acceptance from groups that require personality compromise, encourage your children to initiate activities, gatherings, or projects that reflect their genuine passions. This fosters genuine confidence while attracting compatible people who appreciate their authentic selves.

The Professional Application

In professional contexts, this principle manifests as entrepreneurial thinking—creating opportunities rather than merely pursuing existing ones.

Even within organizational settings, those who create and launch new initiatives typically advance more rapidly than those who merely execute established responsibilities.

The "Wait for Permission" Trap

Most people wait for:

- Invitation before pursuing opportunities

- Permission before implementing ideas
- Approval before expressing authentic interests
- Acceptance before sharing their genuine perspectives

Meanwhile, successful people authorize themselves to:

- Create opportunities rather than wait for them
- Implement solutions rather than waiting for assignments
- Express authentic interests rather than wait for validation
- Share perspectives rather than wait for approval
- Dismiss trends

Individuals with strong self-confidence consciously focus on what aligns with their values, rather than what's popular. Mindlessly following trends can lead to wasted money, time, and a loss of individuality.

Those who wait for permission or invitation often find themselves adapting to suboptimal circumstances rather than creating ideal ones.

The Club Creation Process

- **Step 1: Define Your Values.** Identify your "cool", your "fun", what genuinely matters to you, rather than what you think should matter or what others think.
- **Step 2: Design Aligned Experiences.** Create activities, gatherings, or projects reflecting these authentic values.
- **Step 3: Invite Compatible People.** Share your vision with others who might appreciate similar approaches.
- **Step 4: Maintain Authentic Standards.** Resist the pressure to compromise your vision to attract more participants or gain broader acceptance.

Your Club Creation Challenge

This week, identify one area where you can create rather than seek acceptance:

- **Social**: Organize gatherings reflecting your actual interests rather than joining activities you don't enjoy
- **Professional**: Propose initiatives addressing problems you've identified rather than waiting for assignments
- **Personal**: Establish routines and practices aligned with your values rather than following what's common
- **Family**: Design traditions and activities reflecting your family's unique priorities

Remember: You're not trying to exclude others—you're creating environments where authentic people can connect around genuine shared interests rather than superficial compatibility.

When you create your own club, you attract members who appreciate your authentic leadership rather than demanding you conform to their existing structures.

Principle 32: **The Self-Creation Principle**

Authorize yourself to establish environments aligned with your authentic values rather than seeking acceptance through conformity. Create your own communities, opportunities, and standards rather than waiting for external permission or validation.

◎ Teach & Thrive

Here are five ways to develop self-authorization skills in your children:

1. **Initiative Identification Training:** Develop children's ability to spot opportunities to create rather than just join. Create "Opportunity Spotter" practices where they identify situations that could be better. This builds the skill of seeing possibilities for creation rather than accepting what exists.

2. **Creation-Joining Decision Framework:** Help children decide when to create versus when to join. Create a "Path Chooser" guide with key questions: "Does this fit my authentic values?" "Would creating my own thing work better?" Practice using these questions in real situations.

3. **Micro-Community Building Practice:** Help children practice creating communities. Start with simple "Interest Gatherings" where they identify shared interests and organize small activities, inviting others with similar passions. Provide graduated support that diminishes as their competence grows, eventually transitioning to independent community creation. This teaches them to bring people together instead of always joining others.

4. **Permission-Free Thinking:** Teach children they can create without asking permission first (within guidelines). Identify common "waiting for permission" phrases ("Can I...?" "Am I allowed to...?") and establish alternative self-authorizing language ("I'm going to..." "I've decided to..."). Practice substituting these new patterns in appropriate contexts while maintaining respect for legitimate authority. We told our kids that they don't need to ask as long as: 1. It doesn't hurt them. 2. It doesn't hurt anyone. 3. It doesn't break the house or my things.

5. **Creation Portfolio Building:** Help children recognize and value their ability to create by recording their initiatives. Establish "Creator Portfolios" (digital images are adequate) that capture each environment, opportunity, or standard they establish, rather than merely joining. This builds identity as creators rather than simply participants in others' creations.

Goal: Develop children who naturally create environments aligned with their authentic values rather than compromising themselves to fit into existing structures that don't serve their best interests.

PART 3 SUMMARY

Formula For Success & Freedom

The Strategic Methodology for Building Wealth

Principle 23: You Need to Be an Expert | *The Informed Client Advantage.* Develop sufficient knowledge in domains where you make significant decisions, even when hiring specialists. Your understanding determines quality outcomes.

Principle 24: Dominate | *The Identity Specialization Strategy.* Select and dominate a specific field through concentrated focus. Establish a clear professional identity based on exceptional capability.

Principle 25: A Left-Hand Job | *The Strategic Security System.* Create resilience through backup capabilities and proactive adaptation. Develop immediately employable skills for security and confidence.

Principle 26: Think Long Enough and You Shall Receive | *The Intentional Attraction System.* Utilize clear visualization in conjunction with aligned action. What you consistently focus on with genuine intention manifests through personal transformation.

Principle 27: Formula for Success | *The Universal Achievement Formula.* Success follows a consistent pattern: clearly identify objectives, genuinely desire achievement, and persistently implement the necessary actions.

Principle 28: Take the Bullet Train | *The Mentor Acceleration System.* Dramatically accelerate progress through qualified mentorship and proven pathways. Leverage others' wisdom rather than reinventing everything from scratch.

Principle 29: If You Don't Have This, You Won't Get It | *The Motivational Clarity Principle.* Develop emotionally compelling reasons for your goals. Your ability to persist directly correlates with the clarity and power of your motivations.

Principle 30: Roadmap to Getting RICH | *The Wealth Construction Blueprint.* Follow proven wealth-building progression—skill development, income generation, disciplined saving, and strategic asset acquisition.

Principle 31: Front-Load | *The Front-Loading Advantage.* Tackle challenging tasks first when resources remain strongest. Invest heavily during the early years to maximize the benefit period.

Principle 32: Create Your Own Club | *The Self-Creation Principle.* Authorize yourself to establish environments aligned with your values rather than seeking acceptance through conformity.

Be Better and Achieving Excellence

PRINCIPLE 33

Rewire

> *"The conventional wisdom*
> *is often wrong"*
>
> —*Steven D. Levitt*

If he said that in 2020, he'd probably be canceled on Twitter for suggesting people actually think critically about popular opinions. But the man had a point—most of us sleepwalk through life accepting "wisdom" that's about as helpful as a chocolate teapot.

Here's the thing: some of the most popular advice floating around is actually sabotaging your success. It's like following a GPS that confidently directs you to drive straight into a lake or off a bridge. That has actually happened.

The "Love Yourself Just The Way You Are" Trap

Let's start with everyone's favorite feel-good mantra: "Love yourself just the way you are!"

Record scratch. Freeze frame.

Hold up. If I loved myself "just the way I am" at this moment—sitting here in yesterday's pajamas, having eaten cereal for dinner, with a to-do list longer than a Target receipt—I'd never improve anything.

> **Here's what this advice *should* be: "Love yourself enough to become the best version of yourself."**

There's a massive difference between self-acceptance as a foundation for growth versus self-acceptance as an excuse for stagnation. The person who's chronically late, leaves dirty dishes everywhere, or treats people poorly shouldn't hide behind "that's just who I am."

NO. That's who you're *choosing* to be right now. And you can choose differently tomorrow.

Things you can't change (height, family of origin, past mistakes) deserve acceptance. Things you CAN change (habits, skills, behaviors, mindset) deserve improvement. Learning to distinguish between the two is crucial for both sanity and success.

The Half-Empty Glass Wisdom

Here's another piece of conventional "wisdom" that drives me crazy: "Is the glass half full or half empty?"

Everyone expects you to chirp "half full!" to prove you're a positive person. But here's the plot twist—sometimes "half empty" is actually the smarter perspective.

The "half-empty" person is the one who says, "We need to refill this before we run out." This person is PREPARED. This person is thinking ahead. This person isn't caught off guard when resources dwindle.

The "half full" person might be delusionally optimistic right up until they're thirsty with an empty glass.

A balanced perspective recognizes both current resources and potential needs. It's not pessimistic to prepare—it's intelligent.

The Salary Secrecy Scam

"Don't discuss your salary with coworkers."

This gem comes straight from the employer's handbook, "How to Keep Your Employees Underpaid." Companies LOVE this advice because information asymmetry works in their favor.

But strategic salary sharing among trusted colleagues? That's market intelligence. That's how you discover you're being paid 20% below market rate while your less-experienced coworker makes more because they negotiated better.

Obviously, don't announce your compensation at the company picnic. But refusing to ever discuss salaries with trusted peers? That's like negotiating your worth blindfolded while your employer has 20/20 vision.

The "Eating for Two" Disaster

Speaking of advice that sounds helpful but causes problems—let's talk about "eating for two" during pregnancy. This advice sounds like it came from a handbook titled *Misery Loves Company: How to Keep Your Friends From Ever Fitting Into Their Jeans Again.*

This innocent-sounding guidance has probably caused more gestational weight gain than stress cravings and ice cream binges combined. The truth? You need approximately ONE extra snack per day, not double portions at every meal.

I watched friends apply this "wisdom" and gain sixty-plus pounds, then struggle for years to lose the weight. Meanwhile, the baby needs nutrients, not massive calorie increases.

I myself fell for this lie during my first pregnancy and gained an additional twenty pounds. But I learned and went against this advice for my second pregnancy, bouncing back to pre-pregnancy weight after three months instead of a whole year.

Quality matters more than quantity—but "eat high-quality nutrients for two" doesn't roll off the tongue quite as nicely. As a matter of fact, eat like you have diabetes—choose carefully. You have one body, remember. Actually, you have two to be responsible for.

The Money-Happiness Myth

"Money doesn't buy happiness."

This oversimplification ignores the reality that money buys:

- Healthcare when you're sick
- Education for your children
- Time freedom from financial stress
- The ability to help others
- The ability to be generous
- Experiences that create lasting memories
- Peace of mind during emergencies

Does having money guarantee happiness? Of course not. Does poverty guarantee happiness? Also no. However, money dramatically expands your options for creating circumstances that support happiness.

Neither wealth nor poverty guarantees emotional well-being, but pretending money doesn't matter is just privileged nonsense. People who spread this myth want everyone to stay poor so they feel better about their own situation.

The Rewiring Process

The ability to question conventional wisdom isn't cynicism—it's critical thinking. And in a world where everyone's shouting advice, the ability to evaluate rather than absorb becomes a superpower.

Here's my litmus test for any piece of advice:

- What happens if I apply this entirely?
- Who benefits if I follow this advice?
- What evidence supports this beyond tradition or authority?
- Does this create the outcomes it promises?

Your Rewiring Challenge

Identify conventional wisdom you've been applying unthinkingly and examine it from a different perspective to see if questioning it could improve your life.

Some conventional wisdom earned its status through generations of positive results. Other bits are outdated, self-serving, or never worked in the first place.

Remember: Your job isn't to reject everything—it's to think critically about what deserves space in your brain.

Principle 33: **The Wisdom Discernment System**

Develop the ability to evaluate conventional beliefs based on their practical effects rather than their popularity or tradition. Question common perspectives that may limit rather than enhance your achievement, and choose beliefs that actually serve your goals.

◉ Teach & Thrive

Here are some powerful methods to develop wisdom evaluation skills in your children:

1. **Result-Based Analysis:** Teach children to evaluate advice by looking at the results, asking: "What happens if someone fully applies this?" and "Does this create the outcomes it promises?" Start with age-appropriate examples, such as "Money can't buy happiness" or "You can be anything you want to be." For younger children, use simple scenarios; for older children, explore more nuanced conventional wisdom. This builds the fundamental skill of evaluating advice based on results.

2. **Conventional Wisdom Debate:** Create discussions where family members take opposing viewpoints on common sayings, articulating both supporting and challenging evidence. Make it fun by assigning random positions—even if they disagree with the side they're arguing. This builds intellectual flexibility rather than dogmatic acceptance.

3. **Evidence-Seeking Protocol:** When encountering common advice, investigate whether research supports, contradicts, or qualifies the conventional perspective. For example, research whether the claim "breakfast is the most important meal" is universally valid, or

investigate whether drinking warm water versus cold water actually makes a health difference. This builds the crucial habit of seeking evidence rather than accepting assumptions.

4. **Cui Bono Training:** Help children understand that advice often applies differently across situations rather than representing a universal truth. For example, question who benefits when you're told "low-fat is healthier" (sugar industry) or "you need to take vitamins daily" (supplement companies). Teach them to ask: "Who profits from this advice?" Practice identifying these contextual factors and financial interests behind common sayings.

5. **Personal Testing Experiment:** Help children build confidence in evaluating advice through safe, direct experimentation. Create "Wisdom Tests" where they try different approaches suggested by competing advice. For example, testing whether they study better with or without background music, despite conventional wisdom. Begin with low-risk experiments before progressing to more significant applications. This builds evidence-based rather than authority-based decision-making.

Goal: Raise naturally curious children who question conventional wisdom and think independently—children who evaluate beliefs based on what actually works rather than what's popular and choose perspectives that actually serve their goals.

PRINCIPLE 34

Not Everything Applies 100%

*"The test of a first-rate intelligence
is the ability to hold two opposed ideas
in mind at the same time and
still retain the ability to function."*

—F. Scott Fitzgerald

Fitzgerald clearly never tried to follow parenting advice online. One expert advises "let them cry it out," while another suggests "never let them cry," and yet both cite scientific studies. Meanwhile, you're standing in the nursery at 2:00 a.m., wondering if you're permanently damaging your child or just your sanity.

What Fitzgerald understood that most people miss: wisdom lies in recognizing when principles apply and when they don't. Even the best advice has boundaries, exceptions, and contextual limitations.

The High Standards Paradox

Adhere to our Principle 2, which emphasizes maintaining high standards. Brilliant advice, but what happens when you apply it with the intensity of a perfectionist marine drill sergeant to EVERY aspect of life?

You become the person who rewrites grocery lists three times because the handwriting wasn't perfect, spends forty-five minutes choosing the "optimal" Netflix show, and has a nervous breakdown because the throw pillows aren't precisely centered.

High standards should elevate your life, not paralyze it.

The Front-Loading Exception

Front-loading effort (Principle 31) typically yields excellent results. Attack the most complicated tasks first, complete major work early, invest heavily while young—solid advice across the board.

But what about situations that require adaptive flexibility? Some projects benefit from iterative development, where early perfection might actually backfire.

Take software development. If you front-load by developing all the complex features and building everything according to initial specifications, you might create something users don't actually want. Sometimes the "half-finished, test-as-you-go" approach yields better results than the "complete everything perfectly up front" method.

Similarly, in parenting, front-loading all the advanced principles when the child is only three years old might create rigid systems that don't serve your actual family dynamics.

The Academic-Life Strategy Split

Schools teach valuable lessons, but some academic strategies are precisely the wrong ones for real-world success.

- **Academic Wisdom:** Start with easy questions to maximize points within time constraints.

- **Life Application:** Tackle complex challenges first while your resources remain strongest.

- **Academic Wisdom:** Don't copy others' work—originality is paramount.

- **Life Application:** Many successful businesses adapt proven models rather than reinventing everything from scratch.

- **Academic Wisdom:** Individual achievement matters most.

- **Life Application:** Collaboration and network effects often determine success more than solo brilliance.

The ability to recognize when academic training helps versus hurts real-world performance? That's advanced-level wisdom.

The Future Pacing Pitfall

Manifestation and "future pacing" can be incredibly powerful. Acting as if you already have what you want builds confidence and prepares you for opportunities.

Buying appropriate interview clothes before landing your dream job? Smart preparation.

Buying a bird cage before the bird? Strategic.

Purchasing Lamborghini wheels when you're driving a 2007 Honda and drowning in consumer debt? That's not future pacing— that's Broke Future Pacing.

The principle works when the "acting as if" involves reasonable preparation and mindset shifts. It backfires when it involves financial decisions that assume outcomes rather than prepare for them.

The School Rules vs. Life Rules Reality

Here's where things get really interesting. Many school-taught behaviors that ensure academic success actually limit real-world achievement:

- **School:** Raise your hand and wait to be called on.
- **Life:** Proactively identify opportunities and take initiative.

- **School:** Follow instructions precisely without questioning authority.
- **Life:** Think critically about guidance and adapt strategies to specific situations.

- **School:** Avoid helping others during tests—that's cheating.
- **Life:** Collaboration and knowledge-sharing accelerate everyone's success.

- **School:** All subjects deserve equal attention and effort.
- **Life:** A strategic focus on high-impact areas yields better results than a scattered effort.

This doesn't mean school learning is worthless—just that understanding WHEN those lessons apply and when they need modification for adult effectiveness is key.

The Contextual Wisdom Framework

The ability to determine appropriate application contexts separates sophisticated thinking from blind rule-following. Rather than applying principles uniformly across all situations, develop the discernment to identify when, where, and how specific concepts generate optimal results.

This contextual wisdom develops through experience, observation, and thoughtful evaluation rather than automatic implementation.

Consider advice about being honest. "Honesty is the best policy" works beautifully in most situations—with friends, family, business partners, and yourself. But absolute honesty? That would mean telling your neighbor their new haircut looks like a crime scene, or sharing your unfiltered thoughts about every movie, meal, and meeting.

Context matters. Honesty serves relationships and personal integrity. Brutal honesty without compassion or consideration of timing can damage both.

Your Sophisticated Application Challenge

Even the best advice has exceptions. Identify one that shouldn't be applied in specific situations.

The goal isn't to follow rules mindlessly or reject them altogether. It's to develop the judgment to recognize when principles serve your objectives and when they need modification.

This nuanced approach prevents both dogmatic rule-following regardless of circumstances and the complete abandonment of valuable principles upon discovering exceptions. Instead, you develop the wisdom to determine how specific guidelines apply to particular situations.

Principle 34: **The Application Intelligence Principle**

Develop sophisticated discernment about when, where, and how specific concepts are most effectively applied. Recognize that even the most valuable principles have appropriate application contexts rather than universal implementation requirements.

◉ **Teach & Thrive**

Here are ways to develop contextual application skills in your children:

1. **Principle Boundary Practice:** Help your children understand guidelines by recognizing when they don't apply. For example, "sharing is caring" works well with toys and snacks, but requires modification for personal belongings and is not applicable to passwords or private information. This builds flexible thinking rather than black-and-white rule-following.

2. **Situation-Based Decision Practice:** Help children learn to adjust principles based on the situation. Create "If-Then-But" frameworks for essential principles that include both general guidance and exception conditions. For example: "If someone asks for help, then assist, but not if helping endangers your safety or involves lying."

3. **Principle Modification Practice:** Help children adapt principles to different situations. For example, "treat others the way you want to be treated" may require modification when interacting with individuals who have different preferences or cultural backgrounds.

4. **Outcome-Based Evaluation:** Help children judge whether a principle worked by looking at what happened, not just whether they followed

the rule." Create a simple template with sections for: "What principle was applied," "How it was implemented," "What resulted," and "What adjustments might improve outcomes." For example, reviewing when "figure it out yourself" was the right approach (learning from mistakes and building confidence) versus when stubbornly refusing help created frustration and wasted valuable time. This builds evidence-based rather than dogmatic application.

5. **Context Recognition Training:** Teach children that principles apply differently in different situations. Practice with real examples: "Honesty is good, but is it kind to tell your friend their art is ugly? How could you be honest AND kind?" Use "What if..." scenarios to help them think through when rules have exceptions. This builds judgment and wisdom, not just rule-following.

Goal: Raise children who can think for themselves—not mindlessly following rules or completely rejecting them, but developing the judgment to apply principles correctly for positive results.

PRINCIPLE 35

Be Attractive.
Don't Be Unattractive

"The value of a man
should be seen
in what he gives and not
in what he is able to receive."

—*Albert Einstein*

Success comes to valuable people, not to desperate pursuers. It's like the difference between being the person everyone wants to invite to parties versus the person who shows up uninvited with a bag of gas-station chips.

The beautiful irony is: when you focus on adding value rather than extracting it, you naturally attract more abundance. When you operate from a mentality of giving rather than taking, you become a magnet for opportunities and relationships.

The Value-Creator vs. The Pincher

There are two types of people in the world: Value-Creators and Pinchers.

The Pincher is the person who:

- Gives away items they know are poor quality—not things that simply don't fit or aren't their color, but things they wouldn't want themselves.
- Suggests splitting the bill evenly after ordering the most expensive items.
- Brings food they wouldn't eat while expecting others to bring caviar.

The Value-Creator is the person who:

- Leaves places better than they found them.
- Gives more than they receive in most interactions.
- Makes other people's lives easier through their presence.

The Pincher constantly calculates what they can extract. The Value-Creator continually asks what they can contribute. Which kind of individual is more attractive?

The Intention Behind the Action

The critical distinction between value-creation and pinching lies in intention and transparency.

Giving away unused items to appreciative recipients creates genuine value. Offloading things you dislike while presenting them as thoughtful gifts represents extraction disguised as generosity.

The difference isn't always in the action—it's in the intention behind it and the honesty about what's happening.

Teaching Value-Creation Early

This principle becomes even more powerful when you instill it in your future millionaires early on.

My kids are already learning that we clean up our messes, plus a little extra; we bring something to contribute when visiting others, and we look for ways to help rather than just ways to benefit.

This isn't about creating people-pleasers who never advocate for themselves. It's about building people who naturally add value wherever they go—which makes them incredibly valuable to others.

The World-Class Within Your Context

Being a Value-Creator actually means providing world-class excellence within your specific operating context.

This doesn't mean you need luxury positioning in every scenario. A food truck can deliver outstanding value by serving incredible tacos at fair prices and providing friendly service.

When you help someone, help all the way—provide world-class help and don't just phone it in. A babysitter can be world-class by arriving prepared, keeping kids engaged, and leaving the kitchen cleaner than they found it.

Excellence is relative to context, but it's absolute within that context.

When I host friends for dinner, I'm not trying to compete with three-Michelin-star restaurants. However, I am striving to create the best possible experience within my abilities—offering good food, a clean house, a comfortable atmosphere, and genuine attention to my guests.

The Abundance Multiplier Effect

Here's the magic of value-creation: it compounds exponentially.

When you consistently add more value than you consume, people notice. They want to work with you, hire you, recommend you, and include you in opportunities. Word spreads about your reliability, creativity, and contribution.

Meanwhile, Pinchers also gain a reputation—just not the kind that opens doors.

I've watched this play out countless times in professional settings. The person who always delivers slightly more than promised, who makes meetings more productive, who solves problems rather than creating them—that person gets promoted, gets referred, gets invited to interesting projects.

Your Attraction Challenge

Identify a situation or an area where you can: provide value, offer help, connect others to opportunities, improve someone's life, or perform an act of kindness.

Principle 35: **The Value Surplus Principle**

Consistently create more value than you consume across all environments. Maintain a contributor rather than consumer orientation, ensuring your presence enhances rather than diminishes the resources available to others.

◎ Teach & Thrive

Here are powerful methods to develop value-creation skills in your children:

1. **Value-Added Training:** Teach children to look for ways to contribute and help. Create a "Value Creator" mindset by asking: "How did I make this better?" For younger children, this might involve simple cleanup or organization after playdates; for older children, more sophisticated contributions, such as helping set up when visiting friends. Make this natural rather than forced by celebrating their discoveries of improvement opportunities.

2. **Giving-Taking Balance:** Help children notice whether they're giving as much as they're taking. After a playdate, ask: "What did you enjoy?" and "What did you do to make it fun for everyone?" This builds conscious awareness of giving and taking patterns that often go unnoticed, leading to thoughtful rather than accidental generosity.

3. **Quality In Any Situation:** Help them understand that quality reflects integrity and effort within constraints rather than absolute resource expenditure. For example, a beautifully set table with homemade cookies can convey higher value than a hastily prepared meal. This builds discernment in genuine value creation.

4. **Being Responsible Practice:** Implement "Trusted with Treasures" activities where they receive increasing responsibility for valuable resources (family objects, shared spaces, group materials) with the explicit expectation of enhancement, for example, organizing the game closet more efficiently or creating a better system for sharing art supplies with siblings. This builds a creator rather than a consumer mindset, which is fundamental to wealth building.

5. **Intention-Impact Alignment:** Help children make sure their actions match what they say they want to do. Create "Inside-Outside Checks" to examine whether their stated intentions align with their actual contributions. For example, when they give a toy to their sibling, ask them if they have outgrown it or if it's broken. When they share snacks with their sibling, ask them if they share a good piece or a bad piece. Practice identifying and closing these alignment gaps through honest self-assessment. Teach them to distinguish between genuine generosity and performative giving. This builds authentic rather than manipulative contribution habits, creating sustainable rather than exploitative relationships.

Goal: Raise children who give more than they take—children who make every place better and build reputations as people who add value wherever they go—becoming naturally attractive contributors rather than repellent takers, understanding that abundance flows to those who give generously.

PRINCIPLE 36

Kaizen!

"Spend each day trying to be a little wiser than you were when you woke up. Discharge your duties faithfully and well. Systematically, you get ahead, but not necessarily in fast spurts. Nevertheless, you build discipline by preparing for fast spurts. Slug it out one inch at a time, day by day. At the end of the day—if you live long enough—most people get what they deserve."

—Charlie Munger

I love this quote so much, I want to cross-stitch it on a pillow. Charlie Munger essentially gave us the secret to life in one paragraph, and most people will read it, nod sagely, then immediately return to the "love me exactly the way I am" mindset.

But here's the beautiful truth buried in those words: you don't need to become a different person overnight. You just need to become 1% better than you were this morning. And if you're a parent reading this at 11:00 p.m. after a day that included a toddler meltdown, spilled coffee, and realizing you've been wearing your shirt inside out since breakfast—well, even you can improve by 1%.

The Corporate Kaizen Awakening

I first encountered kaizen during my corporate days when upper management announced we'd be "practicing kaizen to improve delivery and performance." My initial thought? *Great, another buzzword to add to our collection of synergistic paradigm shifts.* Notice that this book is full of corporate terminology.

But then something magical happened. Instead of demanding we revolutionize our entire workflow by Friday, they asked us to find ONE small thing to improve each week. Just one.

That's when I realized: kaizen isn't just corporate speak—it's a life philosophy that can be applied to all areas in life.

The 1% Rule That Rules Everything

Kaizen translates to "change for the better" or "continuous improvement." The Japanese philosophy emphasizes making small, incremental improvements rather than dramatic overhauls. The goal is simple: improve by just 1% each day.

Here's the math that will blow your mind: if you improve by 1% every day for a year, you'll be 37 times better by year's end. If you get worse by 1% each day, you'll decline to nearly zero. The compound effect of tiny changes is absolutely staggering.

But here's the powerful thing about the 1% approach—it's completely doable, even when life is chaos. You can't always find time for a complete life overhaul, but you can almost always find a way to improve something by 1%.

My Personal Kaizen Journey with Exercise

Let me tell you about my relationship with fitness. For thirty years, I had the athletic ability of a melted ice cube. Working out wasn't in my vocabulary—it was more like a foreign language I had no interest in learning.

But at thirty, staring at my "skinny fat" reflection, I realized I needed to change. The problem? I could barely complete half a beginner workout video without wanting to lie down and accept defeat.

So I applied kaizen. Instead of forcing myself to complete entire workout routines, I committed to doing just half of the exercises each day. Just half. That's it.

Day by day, doing that manageable half-workout, something shifted. My stamina improved. My endurance grew. Before I knew it, I was completing full workouts, then adding extra challenges.

Years later, I work out daily AND run regularly—activities that once seemed as likely as me becoming a professional ballet dancer. The transformation happened one tiny improvement at a time.

After gaining forty pounds with my first pregnancy, I could have panicked and tried extreme measures. Instead, I applied the same 1% principle to my postpartum recovery—making tiny adjustments to my diet, and implementing small increases in activity. The weight came off sustainably, and soon I was able to increase to more intense workouts and return to the better version of me.

The Universal Power of Small Changes

The beauty of kaizen lies in its universal application. The 1% rule works 100% of the time, in any situation, for any person, in every area of life. It's like gravity—a fundamental force that applies everywhere:

- **Learning**: One new word in a foreign language daily
- **Relationships**: One small act of kindness for your spouse each day
- **Organization:** Decluttering one small area each day
- **Career**: Reading one article in your field daily
- **Parenting**: Implementing one tiny improvement to your family routine weekly

> The magic isn't in the individual changes—it's in their compound effect over time. Just like water flow reshapes stone over time, small actions transform into massive results.

Why Big Changes Fail and Small Ones Succeed

Most New Year's resolutions crash and burn by February because people try to change everything at once. They want to exercise daily, eat ideally, meditate, learn Spanish, and organize their entire home—all while maintaining their current responsibilities.

Normal humans get worn out and then give up. But 1% improvements? They slip under the radar. They feel manageable, sustainable, even pleasant.

Small changes also build confidence. Each tiny success creates momentum for the next improvement. Before you know it, you're not just practicing kaizen—you're living it.

The Parenting Kaizen Advantage

As parents, we're constantly trying to improve our children, our homes, and our sanity levels. But the pressure to be perfect can be overwhelming. Kaizen offers a more sustainable approach.

Instead of completely overhauling your family's routine, try improving one small element each week. It could be having everyone put their shoes in the designated spot. It could be starting dinner prep five minutes earlier. Maybe it's reading one extra page during bedtime stories.

These tiny improvements compound beautifully. Your children learn that progress comes through consistent small efforts rather than dramatic gestures. They internalize the growth mindset that will serve them throughout their wealth-building journey.

Your Kaizen Challenge

Pick one area where you can improve by 1% each day. Consider areas where you might apply the 1% principle:

- Parenting and kids' routines
- Self-care routine
- Daily knowledge acquisition
- Skill refinement
- Learning a new skill or language—just one word a day or even one word a week
- Process optimization
- Relationship development
- Health enhancement
- Financial discipline

Remember: the goal isn't perfection—it's progress. And progress, even measured in inches, eventually covers miles.

This profound quote encapsulates a crucial principle: consistent, incremental improvement ultimately yields extraordinary results. "Spend each day trying to be a little wiser than you were when you woke up" establishes the fundamental mindset of daily growth. "Slug it out one inch at a time, day by day" is a reminder that if running isn't possible, then walk; if walking is difficult, then crawl and slug until the destination is reached. Even modest daily improvements accumulate into transformative progress over time.

Principle 36: **The Incremental Excellence System**

Implement daily 1% improvements across key life domains. Consistent, modest advancement compounded over time creates extraordinary progress through the power of incremental excellence rather than sporadic transformation attempts.

◎ Teach & Thrive

Here are powerful methods to develop continuous improvement skills in your children:

1. **Daily Growth Tracking:** Teach your children to progress through small advancements. Create a "Better Today" journal where they identify and record one specific improvement made each day—whether in skills, knowledge, habits, or character. For younger children, use stickers or drawings; for older children, written reflections.

2. **Improvement Experiment:** Help children implement and evaluate small changes by having them identify one element to improve, make a modest change, and assess results—for example, organizing their backpack differently or trying a new approach to morning routines. This builds the scientific mindset essential for effective continuous development.

3. **Skill Decomposition Practice:** Help children break big skills into smaller parts they can work on one at a time. For piano, this might include finger positioning, rhythm, note reading, and dynamics. Focus improvement efforts on these individual elements rather than only practicing the composite skill. This builds the understanding that

mastery comes through component refinement rather than merely repetitive performance.

4. **Self-Comparison:** Help children track their own progress instead of comparing themselves to others. Celebrate improvements like "You improved your time by 30 seconds!" instead of "You're faster than your sister now." This builds intrinsic motivation for improvement rather than depending on external validation.

5. **Build Consistency Habits:** Help children to maintain action. Create visual "Consistency Chains" where each day of goal-supporting behavior adds a visible link. This could be a paper chain, marks on a calendar, or digital tracking for older children. Establish clear minimum criteria for maintaining the chain, focusing on consistency. Celebrate milestone chain lengths (7 days, 30 days, 100 days) while emphasizing the process over outcomes. This builds the understanding that consistency ultimately determines achievement more than sporadic excellence.

Goal: Develop children who naturally want to improve a little each day—understanding that small, consistent progress leads to big results over time.

PRINCIPLE 37

Be Better Than the Previous Generation

"Progress is impossible without change, and those who cannot change their minds cannot change anything."

—*George Bernard Shaw*

Every generation builds on the achievements of those before it, reaching new heights not by rejecting the past but by extending it. It's like the ultimate game of intellectual leapfrog, except instead of playground games, we're talking about creating better lives for ourselves and our children.

Aiming to surpass your parents' achievements isn't disrespectful—it's the whole point of civilization. If every generation merely replicated the previous one's accomplishments, we'd still be figuring out fire and wondering if those round things might roll.

The Generational Advancement Imperative

Imagine if Thomas Edison had thought, "Well, Dad made decent candles, so I guess I'll stick with candles too." We'd still be squinting by candlelight and calling it atmospheric.

Or if the Wright brothers had said, "Our father was a fine bishop. Bishop is good enough for us." We'd still be taking boats everywhere and wondering why travel takes so long.

Every innovation, every advancement, every improvement in human civilization came from someone who respected their foundation while refusing to be limited by it.

This principle applies just as powerfully to individual prosperity. Honoring your parents' sacrifices and achievements while strategically exceeding their limitations creates both personal advancement and stronger family foundations for the next generation.

My Parents' Bootstrap Foundation

My parents immigrated with virtually nothing, worked jobs that barely paid minimum wage, and built a modest but stable life through sheer determination. They gave me something invaluable: proof that advancement is possible, a work ethic that doesn't quit, and the immigrant mentality that views obstacles as problems to solve rather than excuses to accept.

However, they also carried limitations from their experience: a scarcity mindset stemming from genuine scarcity, risk aversion due to having so little margin for error, and unfamiliarity with investment vehicles that could have accelerated their progress.

My job isn't to judge those limitations—they made perfect sense given their circumstances. My job is to build on their foundation while addressing the gaps they couldn't fill.

I've exceeded their income level, investment sophistication, and career flexibility. But I've also maintained their work ethic, family priorities, and commitment to education. I kept what served while adding what was missing.

Now my children will inherit both my parents' foundational strengths AND my additional resources—financial, educational, and strategic. They'll have options that my parents couldn't have imagined, while retaining the character traits that made advancement possible.

The Dangerous Gratitude Trap

There's a dangerous mindset that masquerades as gratitude but actually limits growth: "I should be satisfied with what my parents provided. Wanting more seems ungrateful."

Wrong.

Genuine gratitude looks like this: "I'm grateful for the foundation my parents built. Now I'll use that foundation to build something even better, which honors their sacrifice by maximizing its impact."

Your parents didn't struggle and sacrifice so you could replicate their limitations. They struggled and sacrificed so you could transcend them.

The ultimate disrespect to your parents' efforts would be settling for exactly their achievement level when you have access to everything they built, *plus* additional resources, education, and opportunities. And in today's world, everything is at your fingertips.

Enrichment Acceleration

This generational advancement requires continuous self-enrichment. You can't give what you don't have, and you can't teach what you don't know.

I wish my parents had access to these principles when I was young—comprehensive fundamentals for raising wealthy, successful children that would have given me an even stronger foundation. But they did the best they could with what they knew, and now it's my responsibility to pass forward more than I received.

After college, I discovered these five books that have most profoundly impacted my personal development, in the order that I read them:

1. **"Who Moved My Cheese?"** —Essential adaptation principles for changing environments

2. **"Think and Grow Rich"** —Classic wealth psychology and achievement mindset

3. **"The Secret"** —Manifestation principles backed by psychology

4. **"Rich Dad Poor Dad"** —Financial perspective that challenges conventional thinking

5. **"How to Win Friends and Influence People"** —Blueprint for adroitly handling people and situations

These weren't casual reads—they were intensive study sessions that changed how I think, plan, and act. Each addressed essential aspects of achievement psychology and relationship dynamics necessary for exceptional results. I not only read them but also implemented these principles, tested these strategies, and refined their applications to my specific circumstances. Knowledge without implementation is just expensive entertainment.

The Multi-Generational Vision

The beautiful thing about generational advancement is its compound effect. When you exceed your parents' achievements while helping them experience a greater quality of life, you create multiple wins:

- **Your parents** get to enjoy resources and experiences that weren't available during their prime earning years
- **You** get to live at a higher level while honoring their contribution
- **Your children** inherit a higher baseline from which to launch their own advancement

- **Society** benefits from the innovations and contributions that result from increased capability. You gain the ability to be generous. And generosity flows naturally and more easily when you have excess.

I want my children to earn more than I did, invest more intelligently than I did, and create more impact than I did. I also want them to maintain the character, work ethic, and family priorities that made advancement possible.

They'll face different challenges than I faced, just as I faced challenges distinct from those of my parents. But they'll face them with more resources, better education, and stronger strategic thinking.

Breaking the Limitation Cycle

Some parents unconsciously limit their children's ambitions, often saying things like, "Don't get your hopes up," "Be realistic," "Money isn't everything," "We're not those kinds of people," "We can't afford that," or "Be happy with what you have."

This protective instinct makes sense—parents want to shield children from disappointment. However, it often shields them from the possibility as well.

The alternative? Model ambitious goal-setting while teaching resilience in the face of setbacks. Show them that dreams are meant to be pursued, not abandoned preemptively.

This doesn't mean pressure or unrealistic expectations. It means creating an environment where growth is expected, excellence is modeled, and advancement is seen as natural rather than impossible.

As Ronald Reagan said, "Each generation goes further than the generation preceding it because it stands on the shoulders of that generation. You will have opportunities beyond anything we've ever known."

The Honor-and-Exceed Balance

This approach requires a delicate balance: honoring the contributions of previous generations while deliberately surpassing their limitations.

The *honor* part embodies gratitude, respect, and the responsible use of their foundation. The *exceed* part looks like expanded education, strategic risk-taking, and refusing to be constrained by their circumstances.

Both elements are essential. Honor without advancement creates stagnation. Advancement without honor creates disconnection from the very foundation that makes progress possible.

Your Advancement and Breaking-The-Cycle Challenge

Identify areas where you can be better than the previous generation, for example:

- Parenting methods, styles, values, and skills
- Health and food consumption habits
- Financial accomplishment and wealth-building strategies

What are some specific values that you will pass on to your children?

What are some specific mistakes that you will change for your children?

Principle 37: **The Generational Advancement Principle**

Continuously advance beyond previous generations' achievements while honoring their contributions. Combine respect for established foundations with commitment to exceeding inherited limitations, creating both personal prosperity and stronger launching pads for future generations.

◉ Teach & Thrive

Here are some powerful methods to develop generational advancement skills in your children:

1. **Appreciation-Advancement Ritual:** Teach children how to relate to previous generations. Make it a ritual to share stories from grandparents about their challenges, achievements, and dreams. For example, if grandparents worked factory jobs to provide stability, children could honor that sacrifice while exploring career paths that weren't available in their grandparents' era. This builds the crucial balance between respect and progress that prevents either stagnation or disconnection.

2. **Generational Building Blocks:** Help children understand that each generation should build better than the previous one. Create a "Family Foundation" visual where the land represents the opportunities and values your parents established for you. Your job is to build a stronger, taller structure on that land than they could have—and then pass that improved foundation to your children so they can build even higher.

3. **Knowledge Expansion Guide:** Help children grow their knowledge by introducing them to powerful ideas. For younger children, use simplified versions of profound ideas from picture books about

innovation and achievement; for older children, introduce sources with guidance and discussion. This builds a continuous-enrichment mindset, essential for overcoming the knowledge limitations of previous generations.

4. **Sharing Cross-Generational Experience:** Establish a dinner storytelling tradition where you share your experiences and your parents' lessons learned. In our household growing up, dinner time was storytelling central. My parents and aunts shared war stories from Vietnam, family histories spanning generations, my grandfather's fascinating cases as an Eastern medicine doctor, personal triumphs and failures, life lessons, and hard-won wisdom. These stories weren't just entertainment—they passed down values, preserved our heritage, and helped us understand the shoulders we stand on.

5. **Future Foundation Framework:** Encourage children to think beyond immediate achievements and consider what legacy their efforts will create for their own children. For younger children, use simple concepts, such as "What kind of parent do you want to be?" For older children, explore more complex ideas about generational wealth, knowledge transfer, and the preservation of family values. This builds the long-term thinking needed for real advancement.

Goal: Encourage children to surpass the previous generation—achieving more, building greater wealth, creating meaningful impact, and establishing stronger foundations for future generations to exceed.

PRINCIPLE 38

Pass It Forward

"We make a living by what we get,
but we make a life by what we give."

—*Winston Churchill*

Churchill pointed out something profound: the highest expression of success isn't what you accumulate, but what you contribute.

The beautiful paradox of wealth-building: the more you focus on adding value to others' lives, the more abundance naturally flows into your own. And once you've achieved financial freedom, contribution becomes not just possible but essential—it's literally what transforms success into significance.

The Abundance-Generosity Connection

Financial abundance creates expanded capacity for generosity. When your resources exceed your requirements, contribution becomes a natural extension rather than a personal sacrifice.

Counterintuitively, the mindset of contribution often accelerates the journey TO abundance rather than merely following it. People who think in terms of value creation attract opportunities, relationships, and resources that purely self-focused individuals miss.

This progression from scarcity to sufficiency to generosity represents the highest expression of prosperity. You move from needing help to being stable to providing help—a complete transformation that touches lives far beyond your own. The ultimate luxury is the luxury of being able to be generous. Giving away millions of dollars, hundreds of thousands, or even hundreds of dollars beats the strain of needing assistance.

My Mother's Unregistered Philanthropy

Let me tell you about my mother's informal but extraordinary generosity program. Despite living on a modest retirement budget and never dining out or buying non-essentials, she allocates several hundred dollars each year to help older adults in her hometown in Vietnam.

These aren't people with minor inconveniences. These are individuals living in basic shelters with dirt floors and walls patched with scrap metal and straw. They have no employment opportunities, no government assistance, no family, and often survive on a single piece of bread or partial rice bowls. Some days, they skip meals entirely.

My mother coordinates with my aunt in Vietnam to identify those most in need, then provides both direct financial support and necessities like cooking pots. It's not a registered nonprofit with tax benefits and donor recognition—it's just one woman who remembers what hardship looks like and refuses to turn away when she has the capacity to help.

Her initiative inspired my sister and me to contribute. Then I got my husband to join, and now I'm looking to recruit more. We've even discussed establishing more formal assistance programs or soup kitchens. While modest in scale compared to major philanthropic efforts, this project demonstrates how meaningful contribution begins with intention and action, regardless of initial size.

The Compound Effect of Kindness

Small acts of generosity compound just like investment returns. The person you help today might help someone else tomorrow. The child whose education you support might grow up to solve important problems. The struggling family you assist may eventually become stable enough to help others.

My mother has no idea how many lives her modest contributions have touched over the years—not just the elderly adults she helps directly, but the example she set for her children and grandchildren: that contribution is our responsibility.

The few hundred dollars she gave to distant relatives helped create millionaires. That family thrived and gave their children a head start. Those children are now millionaires, and their children have a completely different financial trajectory. And no, I'm not talking about millions in Vietnamese dong—this is after conversion to US dollars.

This ripple effect makes contribution incredibly leveraged—your impact extends far beyond your direct involvement.

Teaching Generosity Intelligently

The goal isn't to create children who give away everything they have— that's not generosity, that's poor financial planning. The goal is to develop children who are grateful and reciprocate to the Universe by giving back. It's not just kindness; it's a duty to pass it forward.

Jean-Jacques Rousseau captured this perfectly: "Gratitude is a duty which ought to be paid, but which none has a right to expect."

My kids are learning that:

- We clean up our messes, plus a little extra.

- We bring something to contribute when visiting others.
- We look for ways to help rather than just ways to benefit.
- We share from our abundance rather than our scarcity.
- We light others' candles—it doesn't dim ours, and in fact, it brightens our path.
- We give strategically to create maximum positive impact.

This isn't about creating social workers with fuzzy feelings. It's about cultivating individuals who understand that their own success enhances their capability for meaningful contributions.

The Strategic Approach to Giving

As your children develop wealth-building capabilities, teach them to approach generosity strategically rather than emotionally.

Emotional giving responds to immediate needs without considering long-term impact or sustainability.

Strategic giving considers questions like:

- How can this contribution create the most positive change?
- What approach addresses root causes rather than just symptoms?
- How can I leverage my unique skills and resources for maximum impact?
- What partnerships or collaborations would multiply the effect?

Both approaches have value, but strategic giving tends to create more sustainable change while building the giver's capacity for continued contribution.

The Three-Life Minimum

Here's my challenge for your future millionaires: commit to meaningfully improving the lives of at least three people beyond your immediate family circle.

Not through massive philanthropic gestures (though those are wonderful if possible, but they're not a luxury many can afford), but through intentional, sustained contributions that create real, positive change for specific people.

This might look like:

- Mentoring someone in your area of expertise
- Supporting a child's education in a meaningful way
- Helping an older person maintain independence longer
- Contributing to a cause that aligns with your values and skills
- Creating opportunities for others through your business or career

The specific form matters less than the intention and follow-through. The goal is to establish contribution as a natural part of success, rather than an afterthought when you've "made it."

The Ultimate Expression of Wealth

True wealth isn't measured by what you can buy—it's measured by what you can give without diminishing your own security.

When you reach the point where helping others doesn't require personal sacrifice, you've achieved something more valuable than any luxury purchase: the freedom to contribute meaningfully to others' lives.

The Full Circle Moment

There's a beautiful moment that comes when your financial education efforts reach fruition: watching your children voluntarily choose generosity from a position of strength.

When they can write a check that meaningfully helps someone without making a dent in their bank account, when they can donate time and skills because their financial systems run smoothly without constant attention, when they can say yes to worthy causes because they've built sustainable abundance—that's when you know the wealth-building education succeeded.

They've learned not just how to make money, but why making money matters—so they can make a difference in their lives and in the lives of others.

Your Passing-Forward Challenge

It doesn't have to be earth-shattering—start by helping one person and returning a favor, either directly to the person who helped you or by paying it forward to someone else.

- What act of kindness or favor did someone do for you that you can do for others?

- Who picked up the tab and made your birthday special? Can you do the same for that person or someone else?

- What opportunity was given to you that you can now provide for others?

- What mentorship can you give to others?

- What positive impact did someone create in your life that you can replicate for others?

Principle 38: **The Contribution Culmination**

As you achieve prosperity, expand your impact through intentional generosity. Transform personal achievement into broader advancement by improving lives beyond your immediate circle, recognizing that meaningful contribution represents the ultimate expression of success.

◉ Teach & Thrive

Here are powerful methods to develop contribution habits in your children:

1. **Generosity Capability:** Teach children to give according to their resources. Show them how giving evolves from making cards and helping others (when young) to giving money from allowance or earnings (when older).

2. **Direct Impact Experience:** Show contribution through firsthand experience. It can be as simple as helping their siblings with a task or letting them assist you with the neighbor's dead car battery. Create age-suitable opportunities where they can witness the direct effects of their assistance. This might involve simple kindness projects with visible outcomes, such as preparing care packages for local shelters, tutoring younger students, or assisting at community events.

3. **Cause Exploration:** Help children discover causes that match their values and interests. Start with local needs they can see, then explore bigger issues as they get older. This builds thoughtful, rather than merely emotional, giving patterns that consider effectiveness and sustainability.

4. **Skill-Based Contribution:** Help children understand how their unique capabilities can create distinctive value through talent-based giving. This could involve utilizing artistic talents (creating decorations for community events) or leveraging academic strengths (tutoring or providing homework help). Match their developing abilities with appropriate service opportunities that feel meaningful rather than burdensome.

5. **Legacy Impact Vision:** Help children understand how their success can help others. Create a "Ripple Effect" exercise where they imagine how their success can impact their lives, their children, and the world. For younger children, use simple examples, such as how helping one child learn to read might enable that child to teach others. For older children, explore more complex concepts about systemic change and its impact. Connect this vision to their wealth-building goals, demonstrating how financial success enhances their ability to make meaningful contributions.

Goal: Raise children to be value-added contributors who create meaningful, lasting impact—understanding that true wealth is measured not by what they accumulate but by what they give, and that passing forward their success represents the ultimate expression of achievement.

PART 4 SUMMARY

Be Better and Achieving Excellence

Achieving Excellence and Creating Legacy

Principle 33: Rewire | *The Wisdom Discernment System.* Question conventional wisdom based on practical effects rather than popularity. Choose beliefs that actually serve your goals.

Principle 34: Not Everything Applies 100% | *The Application Intelligence Principle.* Develop sophisticated discernment about when and how principles apply. Recognize contextual boundaries rather than universal rules.

Principle 35: Be Attractive. Don't Be Unattractive | *The Value Surplus Principle.* Consistently create more value than you consume. Maintain a contributor rather than consumer orientation in all environments.

Principle 36: Kaizen! | *The Incremental Excellence System.* Implement daily 1% improvements that compound over time. Consistent small advancements create extraordinary long-term progress.

Principle 37: Be Better Than the Previous Generation | *The Generational Advancement Principle.* Honor previous generations while deliberately exceeding their limitations. Create stronger foundations for future generations.

Principle 38: Pass It Forward | *The Contribution Culmination.* Transform personal achievement into broader impact through intentional generosity. Meaningful contribution represents the ultimate expression of success.

The Complete Journey

Part 1: Foundation to Cultivate the Seed. Builds the foundational mindset through exposure, standards, gratitude, discipline, vision, self-worth, and confidence. This foundation cultivates the belief that wealth is achievable and the mental framework to pursue it.

Part 2: Fundamental Habits. Installs the daily operating system through productive habits, resourcefulness, efficiency, discernment, strategic relationships, and health prioritization. These automatic behaviors compound daily, creating the infrastructure for long-term wealth building.

Part 3: Formula for Success & Freedom. Provides the specific wealth-building methodology through expertise, specialization, security planning, manifestation, proven formulas, mentorship, motivation, and systematic execution. These fundamentals turn preparation into action with proven systems that create actual financial freedom.

Part 4: Be Better and Achieving Excellence. Achieves excellence through critical thinking, nuanced application, value creation, continuous improvement, generational advancement, and meaningful contribution. The culmination where personal success becomes lasting legacy and positive impact.

THE ULTIMATE GOAL: Raise children who achieve financial freedom by age 40 while developing the character, skills, and mindset to create lasting positive impact in the world.

What's Next?

You've learned the principles—**now it's time to implement them.**

Implementation Checklist & Self-Assessment

Turn insight into action. Download your Implementation Checklist & Self-Assessment at www.momiwillberich.com to track your progress and stay accountable.

Community Connection

Success grows faster in community. Join our implementation Facebook group to connect, share wins, exchange practical strategies, discover resources, and support each other on this wealth-building journey. Access the link at www.momiwillberich.com

Action Card Deck

Bring each principle to life with the Action Card Deck—quick, practical examples to help you apply what you've learned.
Check for availability at www.momiwillberich.com

Recommended Resources

Keep growing. Feed your mind with ideas that build momentum:

- *Who Moved My Cheese?* by Spencer Johnson
- *Think and Grow Rich* by Napoleon Hill
- *The Secret* by Rhonda Byrne
- *Rich Dad Poor Dad* by Robert Kiyosaki
- *How to Win Friends and Influence People* by Dale Carnegie
- *F.U. Money* by Dan Lok

Explore more recommended tools and resources at
www.momiwillberich.com

Acknowledgements

To my husband, Johnny

Thank you for your unwavering belief in me and for encouraging me to write this book. From the very beginning, you saw the value in what I had to say and believed I should share this message with the world. You urged me to speak authentically—even when it meant being bold or unapologetically honest.

You have supported me not only in pursuing this dream but in every aspect of the life we are building together. Thank you for being the provider and protector of our family, and for being my steady source of strength. Your faith in me gave me the courage to bring this vision to life, while you continue to chase your own dreams. For that, I am endlessly grateful.

Thank You, Mother

I want to thank my mother. The lessons she taught me at an early age became the foundation of my success. Above all, she taught me to value myself— because self-value nurtures self-worth, and self-worth builds confidence. She often spoke of real estate, reminding me that it is the cornerstone of building wealth. She often said to me, in words that roughly translate as, "Near ink, you'll be stained; near light, you'll shine"—words that have stayed with me, a constant reminder that the people we choose to surround ourselves with shape not only our path but also our destiny.

My Dear Children, Max and Evelyn,

Always strive for excellence. Set high standards not only for what you achieve but for the person you are. Be someone of value. Choose your friends—and your life partner—very carefully, for they shape your path and alter the trajectory of your life. Aim to be better than your parents, and teach your children to be better than you. Above all, love yourself, believe in yourself, and be the best version of yourself. I love you the most in the whole wide world.

Index

A

Acquisition mindset, 85
Age 40 (financial freedom goal), 269-270
Application intelligence, 296-299
Appreciation (gratitude practice), 27-31

B

Back-up plans (left-hand job), 217-218
Baseline thinking (excellence as standard), 20

C

Celebration Equilibrium, 179-183
Collection/Collecting (wealth-building behavior training), 86-87
Compounding (wealth and habits), 31, 38, 86
Confidence, 54, 60-66, 210, 217
• Confidence Trinity, 60
Contribution (passing it forward), 325-330
• three-life minimum, 329
Conventional wisdom (challenging), 287-291

D

DARE U ID (Distinguish, Ask, Recognize, Evaluate, Understand, Identify), 203
Delayed gratification, 37-38
Diplomatic influence (negotiation skills), 139-143
Discipline, 36-39, 71, 234
• work-before-play, 37, 270
D.O.S.E. (dopamine, oxytocin, serotonin, endorphins), 189-190

E

Efficiency (optimization practice), 100
Emotional control, 149-151, 159
• Count 1, 2, 3 technique, 148-149
Excellence (as baseline standard), 20-23, 304, 309, 317
Expertise (informed client advantage), 107, 199-205, 256

F

Financial freedom, 1-6, 257-261
• achieve by age 40, 269-270
Formula for success (what + want + do), 232-235
Front-loading (work young, enjoy early), 265-271
F.U. Levels (Freedom Upgrade), 259-260

G

Generational advancement, 317-322

H

Habits (habit installation), 71, 74-76, 79-80
• PHI Framework (Prevent, Helps gain, Improve), 75
Health (body as temple), 187-190
High standards, 20-24

I

IBM (corporate standards training), 21-22

J

Journey, 311, 335

Judment (emotional judment), 148-149

Job (A Left-Hand Job), 215

K

Kaizen (1% improvement), 309-313

L

Law of Attraction (manifestation), 223-227

M

Mentorship (bullet train/mentor multiplication), 239-243

Millionaire (cultivating), 10, 44-47, 156, 233

Motivation (WHYs/motivational clarity), 249-250

N

Nice vs. Good (principled strength), 131-135

- **10 Mental Education** (Taekwondo code), 133-134

P

Passive income, 256

PHI Framework (Prevent, Helps gain, Improve), 75-78

Preferences (beneficial shift), 113-116

Price tag concept (self-worth), 51-55

Q

Quality recognition, 19-23, 106, 110-111, 117, 128, 188, 290, 305

R

R.A.I.S.E., 54-55

Relationships (strategic association), 122-126, 129, 145, 235

Resourcefulness (creative problem-solving), 94-96

Roadmap to wealth, 259

S

Seasons of Life (Spring, Summer, Fall, Winter), 268-269

Self-creation (create your own club), 276-278

Self-worth (high price tag), 51-55

Showing off (authentic validation), 179-183

Specialization (dominate), 209-212

T

Teaching children (strategies and practices), see Teach & Thrive section at the end of each chapter

Three-life minimum, 329

V

Value creation (attractiveness principle), 303-305

Vicarious learning (cheapest lessons), 165

Vision (goals and dreams), 46, 226, 228

W

Wealth conditioning (early exposure), 13, 15

Wealth construction blueprint, 256-261

W.E.A.L.T.H. Framework, 86-87

Work-before-play, 273

Worth Statements (self-respect affirmations), 137

About the Author

Summer Pham did not grow up with wealth or a roadmap to financial success. A Louisiana State University graduate, she learned the fundamentals of building wealth by observing the habits and mindsets of successful individuals around her, including her parents' affluent friends. Her journey was guided not by meticulous planning but by curiosity, experimentation, and the occasional hard-won lesson. While serving as a global business consultant for IBM, she was introduced to real estate investing, which became the cornerstone of her wealth accumulation. By starting these habits early—often without fully realizing their power—she became a millionaire by forty, achieving financial independence almost by accident.

Her success demonstrates that extraordinary resources or perfect execution aren't prerequisites for financial freedom. Consistent habits and intentional choices are sufficient.

Summer understands that with awareness and intention, far greater financial freedom is within reach. Her mission is to ensure her children never experience the limitations she once faced—lacking the freedom to choose or missing out on meaningful opportunities. She is determined to give them a head start in achieving freedom of choice, generosity, and true autonomy earlier in life.

Through Mom, I Will Be Rich!, Summer shares the principles that can transform a family's trajectory, creating lasting confidence, abundance, and positive impact for generations to come.

www.ingramcontent.com/pod-product-compliance
Lightning Source LLC
Chambersburg PA
CBHW070907130626
46555CB00001B/30